© Gordon D.S. Maddock 2005
Fuzzy Memories
ISBN 0-9549341-0-5

D1823992

Published by:
Gordon D.S. Maddock
Estudio Campana
Crta: Cuevas de los Medinas 16
Retamar 04130 Almeria Spain
Tel-Fax: (00 34) 950 207 975
email: gordon@elomail.net

Design and production co-ordinated by:
The Better Book Company Ltd
Havant
Hampshire
PO9 2XH

Printed in England

FUZZY MEMORIES

Gordon D.S. Maddock

Fuzzy Memories

INTRODUCTION BY
LORD CONDON QPM DL
Commissioner of Police of the
Metropolis 1993 – 2000

Fuzzy Memories is a delightful book that works for me on a number of levels. Perhaps I should declare an interest first before offering some observations about the book. Gordon and I were members of a six month residential course at the National Police Staff College, Bramshill, Hampshire in 1984 and that is where I first met him. We have met virtually every year since then for a reunion weekend with other members of the course, all of whom have now retired from policing. So I am an admirer of Gordon the man and Gordon the artist.

Fuzzy Memories is a charming miscellany of events, impressions and sketches relating to Gordon's career as a policeman in the Cornwall Constabulary in the late 1950s and early 1960s. It is funny in parts because police work has always been and always will be funny and often surreal. It is poignant and sad because again police work is often sad to the point of Greek tragedy. Above all what resonates with me about this book is its perception and honesty. With a light touch of the pen, or more accurately the computer keyboard and the paintbrush, Gordon evokes the atmosphere and the smell and feel of policing in the fifties and sixties. The day-to-day struggle of young police officers with inadequate pay and conditions doing their best to bring up their families and at the same time they sought to give their best to policing. These hardships are juxtaposed with the exuberance and sense of camaraderie of doing a tough job with colleagues you admired and literally trusted with your life.

The book benefits from Gordon's personal charm and sense of duty and his artist's eye for detail. It is also an important contribution to the history of policing because it feels right and true. As a former policeman I feel happy to validate the mood and truth of the sort of events described in the book.

Enjoy the book for what it is. One former policeman's honest and accurate reflections of a serendipity of events which convey the atmosphere of a period of policing during which the bond between the police and the public was at its strongest. The strength of this bond was due to the calibre of the men and women described in this book.

Lord Condon QPM DL
Commissioner of Police of the Metropolis 1993 – 2000.
Kent 2004

ABOUT THE AUTHOR

The author, Gordon D.S. Maddock is a Devonian by birth and a west country man at heart! Now an artist, retired and living in Spain, he has had plenty of time to recall those 'Fuzzy Memories' of happy times spent in the Cornwall Constabulary.

He joined the Metropolitan Police in 1956 transferring to the Cornwall Constabulary in 1958. He remained there as a constable until 1965 when he was promoted to sergeant upon transfer to the Wiltshire Constabulary. The book covers the seven years as Police Constable and Detective Constable number 97 in the pre-amalgamation days of the 'old Cornwall Constabulary'.

Following eighteen years in the Wiltshire Constabulary holding the ranks of Detective Sergeant, Detective Inspector, Chief Inspector, Detective Chief Inspector and Superintendent he moved east to Surrey. There he became a Divisional Commander.

In 1985 he returned westwards to the now amalgamated Devon and Cornwall Constabulary as an Assistant Chief Constable, retiring in 1987 after thirty-one years' police service.

In retirement, he became a consultant to an international computer company and a Security Team Advisor and organizer for the Atlanta Committee for the duration of the Centennial Olympic Games in Atlanta in 1996.

Fuzzy Memories is his first book. It is partially historical, partially anecdotal, yet factually and humorously illustrated by the author's own recollections, illustrations, photographs, sketches and cartoons.

Gordon D.S. Maddock
October 2004

FUZZY MEMORIES

This book is dedicated to my children, Nicola, Fiona and Alistair and in memory of their mother, my late wife Cynthia, who played such a supportive role during the years of my police career.

It is also dedicated in memory of the late Detective Sergeant Norman John Arscott, to whom I owed so much in my formative years as a police officer and to all the members of the then Cornwall Constabulary.

I thank Fiona, my present wife, for inspiring and encouraging me to write this book for all to read.

"When constabulary duty's to be done - to be done,
The policeman's lot is not a happy one - happy one."

William Schwenk Gilbert 1879.

"But they can be...."

Gordon D.S. Maddock PC 97
Cornwall Constabulary 1958

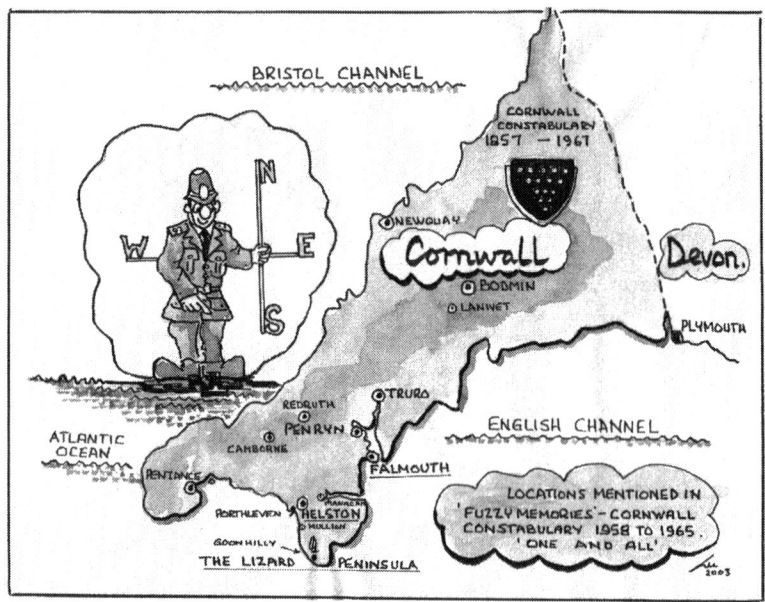

Locations mentioned in Fuzzy Memories

FUZZY MEMORIES

INTRODUCTION BY AUTHOR

The concept for this book has been in my mind for many years. When I decided to join the Police Service, I had no idea that my time spent in the Cornwall Constabulary would be so rewarding.

The Cornwall Constabulary was founded in 1857 and amalgamated with the Devon Constabulary in March, 1967 to form the Devon and Cornwall Constabulary. In 1958, just before my 22nd birthday, I transferred to the Cornwall Constabulary from the Metropolitan Police which I had joined in October 1956.

I never intended becoming a police officer when I left school in 1954. My chosen career was to be an architect having achieved a place at London University. However following two years National Service in the Royal Air Force I realised that being a 'team player' was more my scene than being bound to an office environment for life.

It was whilst waiting for a train on an underground station in London that I saw the recruiting poster for the Metropolitan Police. Having just read and enjoyed a book on the life and work of Bernard Spilsbury, a pathologist, I concluded that crime solving involving the use of forensic science might be an interesting alternative career.

Having visited the recruiting office, I joined the Metropolitan Police knowing that first I must start at the bottom of the ladder as a constable and hopefully, enter the Criminal Investigation Department at a later date. I was prepared to take that gamble and I achieved my ambition and more and never looked back.

Why then the transfer to a constabulary? I was a single man

in London, enjoying the city life, the theatres, the buzz of the city. During one night duty, I looked at a tall block of flats and asked myself, "What if I get married one day and want to raise a family – do I really want them living in a city?" I was a 'Devon boy' and the rural life was my natural environment. At that time, I had a girlfriend in Cornwall and my parents still lived in Devonshire, so I opted to transfer to the Force furthest away from London in the hope that they might accept me. Had they not, then I would have progressed my applications eastwards in the hope that one of the southern counties would consider my application for a transfer.

I had completed my probationary period and grounding in beat duties in the city at Hammersmith and Chiswick with seconded duties to big events in the West End of London. I enjoyed every minute of that period, but long term, I knew and felt that the countryside was calling me to return.

I wrote a letter to the Chief Constable of the Cornwall Constabulary, Richard Bonnar Matthews. He was one of the Trenchard Scheme of Chief Constables who had started his career in the Metropolitan Police. I felt that with my grounding and educational qualifications and coming from the west country, Cornwall might just be interested in me!

The response was positive and I was granted an interview. I travelled to Bodmin to their old granite manorial style headquarters built in 1867. I went by train from London. I was a lone applicant and duly appeared before the Chief Constable and his Assistant Chief Constable, Kenneth George Julian. After stating my case and making it clear that I was not just looking for a quieter life in a County Force and an escape from London and had a genuine desire one day to become a detective, they accepted me by letter received on the 9th April, 1958 and the transfer was arranged. One or two commendations from the Commissioner for apprehending those engaged in larceny in London and my record of service

Richard Bonnar Matthews
Chief Constable 1958

Cornwall Constabulary
Athletic Club Badge

Cornwall County Constabulary

Tel: Nos. 262/4

CHIEF CONSTABLE'S OFFICE,

BODMIN,

9th April, 1958.

Dear Sir,

    With reference to your attendance at this Office
yesterday I am prepared to offer you an appointment in the
Cornwall Constabulary.

    I am today writing the Commissioner of Police asking
if it will be convenient for you to commence duty here on
the 28th April, 1958.

    The Chief Constable ha s decided that your period of
probation will be extended for 12 months from the date of
your joining the Cornwall Constabulary. Please let me know
as soon as possible whether or not you will be able to
transfer on the 28th April.

                    Yours faithfully,

P.C. 331 F. G. Maddock.
Ravenscourt Section House,   Assistant Chief Constable.
3 Paddenswick Road,
Hammersmith.

LONDON W.6.

Letter of acceptance April 1958

to date must have helped convince them I was worthy of consideration!

I returned to London and one month later packed my belongings from the Section House room at Ravenscourt Park which had been my home for my time in the Metropolitan Police and set off on my train journey westward to Cornwall.

I was met at the railway station at Bodmin Road by Sergeant Gordon Harrison, a tall lean man with a distinctive air and poise. He was smart and looked at me with a discerning look as I had travelled on the overnight train from Paddington and appeared a little travel worn and dishevelled. I was ushered to an awaiting, highly polished Austin Seven car, obviously the pride and joy of the equally smart sergeant. We drove the short distance to Bodmin and I remember the smell of the fresh, green spring countryside and felt no doubt that I had done the right thing at least health wise in leaving the London smog behind me.

Being a Devonian, I understood the language of the Cornishman – or I thought I did! No more Cockney twang – just that west country singing Celtic tone that was mellow and welcoming to the ear. I was soon kitted out with the accoutrements and uniform of a county constable and given the number 97. The previous holder of that number had recently been promoted to a sergeant and posted to St. Agnes. I was later to meet him and grew to admire his astute policing methods and devotion to his section. That number served us both well!

A few days of familiarisation at Force Headquarters, a quaint old building of small rooms and elderly occupants soon enabled me to understand the requirements of a county constable. Because of my previous experience in London, the Chief Constable agreed that I need not complete the full two years probation period for all entrants to the force. In my case it was to be reduced to one year. I would attend probationary

Police Constable 1958

Detective Constable 1960

Assistant Chief Constable 1987

lectures at Camborne and would be tutored with the local probationers by Chief Inspector Sivell. A giant of a man by Cornish standards with a voice to match!

I was posted to Falmouth after my introductory days at Force Headquarters, a day's train journey from Bodmin on a line laid by I.K. Brunel. Over viaducts and along steep embankments, the train conveyed me and my baggage to Truro where I had to change and await the branch line connection to Falmouth. Once at the station at Truro I recollect that my travelling friends also had kitbags and multiple items of baggage. They were not to become police constables but were merchant seamen joining their ships in the busy shipping port at Falmouth.

No one met me at Falmouth railway station and I obtained a taxi to the police station. "Where'm you from then my 'ansome? Been in trouble 'ave e?" I assured the driver whom I was later to meet on many occasions when in my uniform, that I was not in any bother, but had come to assist the local police ridding the town of those who had! We became great pals and whenever assistance was needed, the taxi drivers were always there to help as I will later explain.

I was greeted at the police station by Sergeant Roy Grigg. He was an Administrative Sergeant, slightly asthmatic – doubtless the reason for his office role. He was a caring man, softly spoken and inquisitive as to my reason for wanting to join an elite band of men in the Cornwall Constabulary. We got on well in future years and he introduced me to the Cornwall Constabulary Male Voice Choir which I immediately joined.

I was allotted a space in a small cubicle on the third floor with two other occupants, one a police cadet and a probationary constable, David Matthews. We became good friends and shared many on and off duty experiences in the months to come.

I was introduced to my fellow single officers in adjoining cubicles and to other members of the station as they appeared

Falmouth Police Station 1958

for duty. The Superintendent interviewed me with enquiring tones and questions as to my transfer. It appeared that some previous transferees had escaped the Metropolitan Police and other forces for the sun, sea and sand of the Cornish beaches and not to give of their all to policing! Superintendent Charles Brown was a devoted Cornishman, tall, proud and with the air of authority one expected of someone holding that respected rank. A Superintendent of Police was looked up to by the community in the fifties as were most members of the local and county police. The reasons were simple – they served their community and there was mutual respect and communication. I will touch on this aspect in later chapters.

Having met all the staff at Falmouth, I was placed on a duty rota and my policing days in the Cornwall Constabulary were about to begin. I was duly sworn in before the Chairman of the Magistrates, Mr George Ennor and I was now a member of the Cornwall Constabulary.

What followed will be the subject of this book. I will endeavour to recollect as best I can the incidents that I remember 'to the best of my ability' during my days in Cornwall– hence the title – *Fuzzy Memories* and its association of the slang phrase "The Fuzz" for members of the police service. I will also endeavour to capture the structure, principles and procedures within the police service in the fifties and early sixties for historical record. Some officers' names can be remembered and mentioned, some have been forgotten. Of the 400 plus force I admired the devotion of all those who served the people of Cornwall at that time – I was proud to be one of them.

I hope that what follows, amuses, entertains and at the same time, records that part of my life in the police service that gave me great pleasure and pride to be a member of the original "All for one and one for all" – Cornwall Constabulary.

I have included cartoons I drew whilst serving at Falmouth, both for my own entertainment and for that of others. There are also pen and ink sketches of places in and around the town that fascinated me. Some newspaper reports and other items included in the book have travelled with me during my career and retirement, living in fourteen different houses where they were stored unopened in boxes till this day! I had no idea why I was keeping them – until now!

CHAPTER 1

CONSTABULARY DUTIES TO BE DONE!
FALMOUTH

My first day of duty in the Cornwall Constabulary.

It was the 5th of May, 1958, my birthday and I was twenty-two years of age.

PC 97

That day at Falmouth was my first day wearing the uniform of a constable in the Cornwall Constabulary. It commenced with a foot patrol and general familiarisation with Sergeant Jimmy Jackson. Jimmy was a ruddy faced, well-built family man who proudly wore the stripes of a sergeant. A rank very much respected in the fifties and no one called a sergeant any other than full 'Sergeant'. The 'OK Sarge' from the

Metropolitan days had to be forgotten, down in Cornwall each rank was still cherished in the disciplinary structure of the service.

Armed with a new and empty notebook, a 'damage only' and an 'injury accident' book in a leather wallet, with cape over shoulder, handcuffs and truncheon well concealed in trouser pockets, I set out to meet the people of Falmouth. No radio, only a chrome plated whistle on a chain to summon assistance should that be required.

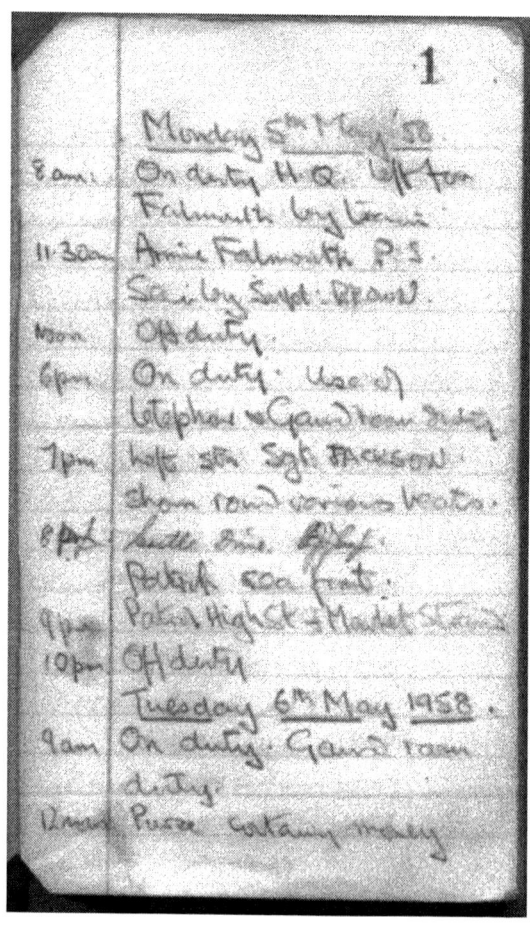

*Pocket book –
day one. Notes made
at the time!*

Each duty was performed in an 8 hour shift 6am to 2pm, 2pm to 10pm and 10pm to 6am. Special duties would be superimposed when events required extra manpower or there was a glut of officers parading for duty.

It rained the first day and my new highly polished boots were put to the test. We stopped to talk to the taxi drivers on the rank in the Moor. Any useful information for that day the sergeant told me, would be coming from them as far as he was concerned. Here there was mutual trust. The taxi drivers were the mobile ears and eyes of the town. "OK boy," he said, "all's quiet according to them – let's go down the street and see what's about." Arwenack Street and Church Street were the two main shopping streets. High Street had a few shops, but was never as busy as the other two. "Problem is boy – lorries do park doubled up – that do cause 'ell in the summer. All they 'grockles' with their cars gets upset that they can't get to beach."

"Right Sergeant," I said. "So we move them on do we?"

"Well boy," he said, "this ain't the Met. Just warn 'um first and use a bit of tact – that's best for all – no unnecessary paperwork!"

We strolled on in the centre of the busy narrow streets and alleyways, locals and shopkeepers bidding us good day and Sergeant Jackson stopping to enquire how the fishing had been off Black Rock the night before. I was soon to learn that he had come from a fishing village on the Land's End peninsula and had been a fisherman before he joined the Penzance Borough Police which had amalgamated with the Cornwall Constabulary in 1947.

"Are 'e interested in fishun boy?"

"Yes" – I said, "I enjoy beach casting."

"No" – he replied, – "real fishun, with a boat."

"Well," I said, "I'll give it a try." From that moment on – we enjoyed each other's company and I had said the right thing. I was shown the spot where to catch prawns on night duty off Fish Strand Quay and from the Town Quay; where to put out lines and recover them before going off night duty – and so on – I became an expert sea fisherman.

I learned a great deal from Sergeant Jackson, the essential role and link between police and public. Something that was slipping away in London when I left. The change and the reward was most welcome as policing was all about prevention in those days – and it worked because of the two-way communication with the public. Only when necessary, was the law enforced and pro-active measures taken. Usually, just a word from an officer in uniform was enough and arrests were few and far between. When the law was broken and a recorded verbal warning adequate, that was the normal course of action. When the law was broken and the need arose to report an offender, reports were submitted and the Inspector would

Falmouth Harbour 1958

How I saw my lot!

recommend summons, a caution or no further action. This would then pass to the Superintendent who would invariably endorse the recommended action to be taken. The reason being that the latter was also the prosecutor in the Magistrates' Court and only cases serious enough to warrant court proceedings would be prosecuted by him. Anything likely to result in a 'Not Guilty' verdict would seldom be taken to court in summary offences! Indictable offences of a serious nature would always be referred to the court for the Magistrates to decide whether they should deal with the matter or refer the case to the Quarter Sessions or Assize Court if the legislation demanded that course of action and the evidence to prosecute was adequate.

The Inspector would also prosecute summary offences or request a remand in police custody if circumstances indicated further enquiries were necessary.

There was a close link between the police, the Clerk of the Court and the Magistrates. The Clerk was much respected and his views and advice taken by both police and the Magistrates when required.

There were two other sergeants at Falmouth when I arrived. Sergeant Bill 'Bilko' Dyer – (the one depicted in my first cartoon!) – and Sergeant 'Sugar' Roberts. Bill was a flamboyant, big man with moustache to match his personality. Many were moved on by his gut alone! If that failed – the cape seemed to do the trick! His presence on a night shift when the pubs turned out could be a reassuring asset. He herded the drunks from the main streets to the docks like a well trained collie! Never were arrests made unless damage was caused or injuries inflicted. In those days, Falmouth was a flourishing and very busy seaport. The pubs did big business from the merchant seamen of all nationalities that came ashore or staggered to and from the docks. With a large dry dock, many spent long periods in the port and the regular drunks would

Town Quay – Falmouth 1958

soon be identified and despatched by taxi back to the dock gates.

Taxi drivers did a good trade and I soon realised why they assisted the police. With a policy of no police intervention other than to keep the peace, the taxi was the only form of transport that police could summon to convey drunks to the docks. It worked and both parties benefited. No sergeant wanted a prisoner to vomit in his personal and private vehicle! No officer wanted to clean out a dirty cell! Common sense prevailed.

Falmouth was a divisional station but there was no official police transport at Falmouth assigned to divisional duty. The only mobile assistance within the division being a motorcyclist and rider for the despatch of messages. One divisional motor car and one divisional motorcyclist were based at Falmouth but came under the control of the Traffic Department at Force Headquarters in Bodmin. They could be used anywhere within

A 'Point' at Church Steps – Falmouth

the county. The local Superintendent had prior demand on these vehicles based within his division for special occasions or events, but they did not get involved with the local day-to-day caseload shared amongst the foot patrol officers. I had been used to squad cars, traffic cars, motorcyclists by the score in London and now – nothing official to call upon for support and nothing with a radio! All communication was made by 'making a point' at a public telephone box or by the Sergeant meeting you at a pre-determined place at a set time allocated when you paraded for duty. This meant that a tour of duty was choreographed, each step measured and points allocated to fit the eight hour period. The town area was large and had numerous beats. Some small and others large. One thing was certain, with no transport you soon became very fit walking in excess of ten miles during a tour of duty in all weathers! One refreshment break of forty-five minutes and return to the station was permitted – all other breaks were 'unofficial' and either resulted in good information being gleaned or the

Looking towards Pendennis Castle Falmouth

prospect of being reported for 'loitering and talking unnecessarily' on duty! Even in the late fifties – the rule book was very antiquated! The policy was to use the café or tea stop that the Sergeant used!

The third sergeant was 'Sugar' Roberts. He was a small man, quiet, dark swarthy complexion and always ready to assist. He enjoyed the office work, the preparation of the duty sheets, the general running of the station and supervision of internal matters. His quiet manner taught me a great deal as his interview technique often brought results where other methods failed. He was exceptionally good with juveniles – the main offenders even in those days! His nickname came from his liking for spoonfuls of sugar in his tea. The enquiry office man always made the tea and never forgot the sugar requirement where Sgt. Roberts was concerned.

Each sergeant was permitted to use their own car for duty purposes, collect and convey prisoners, and visit PCs on supervision liaison. Each liaison would be recorded both by the PC and the Sergeant who would initial the officer's pocket book. For the use of their private car, they were paid a mileage allowance with an additional rate for passengers carried. It was

Detective Sergeant Norman J. Arscott

amazing how readily a sergeant would offer a lift when the end of the month allowance was within budget! Their initials became very frequent in one's pocket book at remote locations towards the end of the month!

The Inspector met me on my third day and first day alone on patrol. I was walking along the street and this tall, impressive man in Inspector's uniform appeared from the doorway of a hairdressing salon. I was now to meet Inspector Doug Bassett for the first time. "Welcome to Falmouth son," he said. I immediately sprung to attention and saluted. He returned the salute and said that whilst he appreciated the gesture – such action was not always required. "Depends on the circumstances see." I got the message! We met again on numerous occasions as he lived next to the police station in the house at the bottom of Quarry Hill. An adjoining door led from his house into the station and when on 'guardroom' duties (station duties – enquiry office) he would appear in part civvies and part uniform to tell you that he was now getting near the end of his career and things weren't like they used to be! He praised good work and soon identified the slackers in the station.

My attention had been drawn to another sergeant, a bit of a legend I was told. He was the only Detective Sergeant with a regular team of two Detective Constables with offices on the first floor. We seldom went there unless called in from 'time off' to explain why we hadn't found a forced entry to a premises during our night shift tour of duty! As I then lived on the top third floor of the station, I often heard this booming voice and smelt the pipe smoke wafting upwards towards our quarters. This was the man I had to impress if I wanted to be a detective! I didn't really know what to make of him at first, but with time I soon respected his methods and success as a detective. He was Norman John Arscott – the legend that I was to work with two years later and never forget!

CHAPTER 2

DAILY ROUTINE

The shifts changed, the duties and work were as varied as the Cornish weather and I gradually passed through my year's probation. I made arrests, I reported people to be summoned to Court for their misdemeanours, I enjoyed the company of my fellow officers and I began to make friends in Falmouth. When off duty I would paint and draw local scenes as I had always been interested in art, and still am! I owned a Lambretta scooter for transport which I kept in the Inspector's garage at the top of Quarry Hill and when not living in 'my cubicle' on the station, I would make the most of what Cornwall had to offer and travel far and wide. I had one or two girlfriends as I was still single. There was Joy from Marks and Spencer,

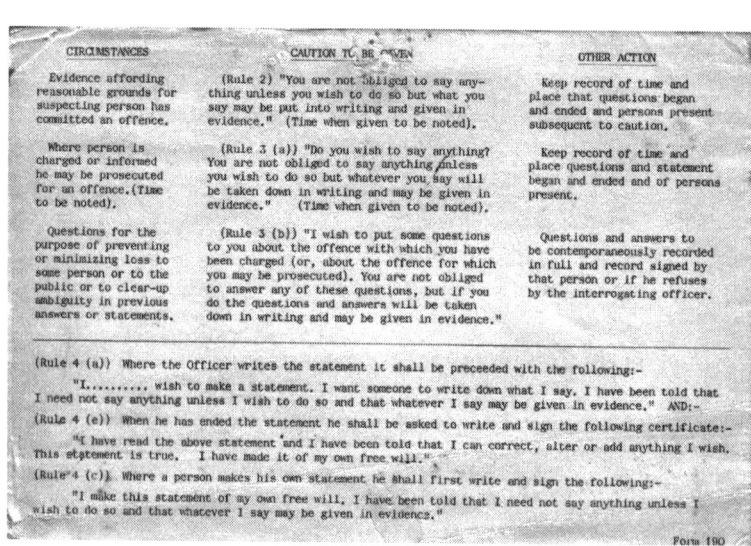

The official caution!

Caught fishing!

Brenda – the secretary at the Girls' Grammar School and I sometimes saw my first Cornish girlfriend, Elizabeth, whom I had met when I was on holiday in Penzance during my National Service. We had drifted apart due to distances and she had found another boyfriend. I had no shortage of both male and female friends in this quaint old Cornish town!

Being single was no problem. Meals were not a problem! Keeping the weight down was! We had a cook who would come in daily and cater for the needs of all the single men and prepare the prisoners' meals when required. She was a large, mature lady who doubled as 'matron' when there were female prisoners to care for. Mrs Jewell was the wife of a tug captain and knew how to cook. Her meals were true Cornish fare. The Cornish pasties were larger than dinner plates and often hung over the edge of the plate by inches! One PC – Phil Simmons loved his food and if you didn't get into the refreshment period on time – maybe it would all be gone! I once saw him eat six fried eggs, bacon, beans, toast and sausages before turning in for a sleep after night shift! The roast dinners were the best I ever tasted and always served with a smile except to those who left the kitchen dirty. They caught the full wrath of a force nine gale when they next appeared.

To be alone walking in the borough of Falmouth in the middle of the night gave one time to think and reflect on life. My favourite beat included Pendennis Castle, a location I would often return to when off duty to sketch. With my love of architectural buildings, this one fascinated me. Whatever time of day or night, I never felt fear or lonely. I knew at times I might be only one of two officers on night duty – the other officer could be miles away and certainly not within whistle blowing distance! (It's a bit like having a whistle to blow to attract attention when your aircraft has just ditched in mid-Atlantic!) The Sergeant would be in the police station with the

Pendennis Castle Falmouth

'guard room' officer who would man the enquiry desk, visit prisoners and answer the telephone. The latter machine was an antiquated piece of equipment with a multitude of cables that had to be pulled from the base and linked to a vast array of sockets denoting the required office or extension. To call the extension, one would wind a handle with vigour to generate enough electricity to ring a distant bell. A flap would then fall to indicate that the call had been connected. Pulling out the wrong cord would result in angry insults from the recipient who had been erroneously disconnected. Making a point was the only way that the Sergeant could contact you and establish that you were still intact and "all was quiet" – a phrase I will never forget.

There was an emergency call system from the manual telephone exchange of the then GPO direct to the divisional police station. A special red flap would fall and the operator would connect the caller to the guardroom PC and pass details. Invariably, the Sergeant would then take his car, pick up the nearest or first located officer and attend. Response time was remarkable and far quicker than today's automated and co-ordinated and computerised command control systems. The reason being that very few dialled 999 unless it was a real emergency. Most calls from the public were received on the normal police station telephone number. The public were reluctant to use the 999 system for fear of troubling their constabulary unnecessarily. To call the police was a last resort and early intervention by police went against the grain of Cornish pride to resolve their differences themselves. Only serious matters came to our attention.

We seldom, if ever patrolled in pairs. The establishment of some twenty-five available officers split into shifts and allowing for days off (Rest Days) didn't allow that eventuality. A sergeant would often be accompanied by a constable for part of a late shift or early night shift foot patrol. That was the only time you could expect immediate assistance should something arise.

It was during an early afternoon patrol of the busy town area that I made my way to the Town Quay. Pleasure boats plied the Fal and Helford rivers from this quay and it was often busy and an area of congestion. As I walked down towards the quay, I saw a large group of people shouting and cheering beneath the Harbour Master's office. The area was packed with holidaymakers, locals and fishermen. A customs officer told me that there was a bad fight taking place and "things were pretty ugly." I pushed my way through the crowd and as I got nearer to the two men fighting I could see that they were two Pill brothers. Both were characters, slim and wiry yet not without the ability to inflict serious harm to themselves and others. Someone told me that one had a knife. I thought little of this as most fishermen and boatmen carry knives. I knew both of them and had spoken to them on many occasions. The

The scene of the fight!

immediate thought that went through my head was that the crowd expected me to do something about it! They were all looking at me – so I had to act. I tried to get them to stop but neither would heed my instructions. One was more aggressive than the other and I chose to arrest him. I stepped in and arrested him, the crowd cheered and I marched him through the streets to the police station, some 500 yards away. On arrival at the police station, Sergeant Jackson met me as someone had made a phone call and he was about to leave the station and make his way to the quay. I told him I had arrested one of the men for his conduct in a public place. Falmouth had many bye-laws as well as the legislation covering Public Order. The sergeant accepted the charge and told me that no one had arrested a Pill brother before. The matter was dealt with and the next time we met on the quay – the offender shook my hand and stated that he would not fight again!

To my amazement, the Inspector called me into his office the following day and told me that the phone call received at the station after I had made the arrest had come from a friend of his at Taylor's Garage offices, overlooking the quay. From what the Inspector had been told, my actions had earned the praise of the locals. The Inspector was impressed and my record suitably endorsed. A simple incident – yet one that sticks in my memory and one that could have gone so horribly wrong.

All events and incidents were recorded in an officer's notebook which would be examined and initialled at the end of a tour of duty by the Sergeant as would all liaisons during the shift. Any incident other than an accident or a crime, which had special report procedures, would be the subject of an entry in the Occurrence Book kept on the Enquiry Office counter next to the Charge Sheet Register, the Crime Complaint book and the Lost and Found Property book. Other books recorded Lost and Found Dogs, issue of Pedlars' Certificates, use of Temporary No Waiting signs and Key Holders of Business

Premises. There were no technical aids and everything would be handwritten in the various books and registers. Typewriting skills were essential for Crime Reports and Incident Reports, Summary Offence Reports and other Incidental Reports requiring decision or further action. Most typing would be done in an officer's own time or during the night shift or after the official tour of duty and seldom would overtime be recorded. No overtime was paid for but time off would be granted in certain cases if 'the contingencies of duties permitted'.

CHAPTER 3

LOVE AND MARRIAGE!

The devotion to duty was a normal and accepted 'service' aspect of police work in Cornwall in the fifties. This accounted for the very high detection rate for criminal offences and the availability of manpower when circumstances demands. Often incidents would be investigated by those on duty together with those volunteering to assist in their own time. This was especially the case with single men living on the station. If a child or elderly person was missing there was no difficulty in getting volunteers to join the hunt. Most police work was done on foot and in immediate contact with the general public. There was no radio, mounted branch, marine division, helicopter support unit – just man-hours, communication by word of mouth and the local press. More about them later.

Time spent in general uniform duties as a PC gave me a great respect for the public and their co-operation in assisting the police: something I never forgot during the remainder of my career. Tact and good humour were essential ingredients in de-fusing many situations that today would result in Riot Squads or Special Tactical Groups being called. The real threat to the officers was often self-induced if it ever arose and I believe that to be the case today. Officers were in the main more mature in age and service and knew their public. Many were ex-servicemen and deserved the respect they got when they became police officers. In the late fifties, the PC establishment consisted of half 'mature' officers both in age and service and younger men who had not been required to do National Service. The former taught the latter the tricks of the trade. There will always be the isolated incident when special procedures are required. Many incidents I witnessed or heard about later in my career were often fuelled by lack of communication on the part of the police or aggressive handling of an incident in the earlier stages by inexperienced and over zealous young officers.

Sgt. Roberts once told me that once a call is received, never rush to the scene. It will either be over when you arrive or those involved so exhausted that the job of the police made easier. I remembered that advice and it was good advice. (I was on motor patrol at the time and gave him a lift! I think he didn't appreciate my police driving being put to practice!) More about motor patrol and traffic duties later!

Many night duties in the 'guard room' when there were no prisoners to visit left time for study as Falmouth was quiet after 1 am. It was during those hours that I typed up many of my reports and examined other aspects of policing with a view to taking my promotion examinations. The promotion examinations were divided into two parts in those days: an educational part and police subjects. The former was a Civil Service examination and covered Maths, English and General Knowledge, the latter assorted police subjects. A higher mark obtained in the former examination ensured a pass to inspector level whilst a pass mark ensured qualification to the level of sergeant. You could take these examinations each year after five years' service until qualified for promotion to sergeant. Having qualified, you then awaited selection based on performance. Most would wait about eight years on average for promotion from PC to sergeant.

I was not yet qualified to sit the examination with four years' service, but made the most of keeping up to date with ever changing legislation.

It was during one such quiet night that I received a telephone call whilst on guardroom duty that was to change my life and status. A lady telephoned and asked to speak to a fellow officer.

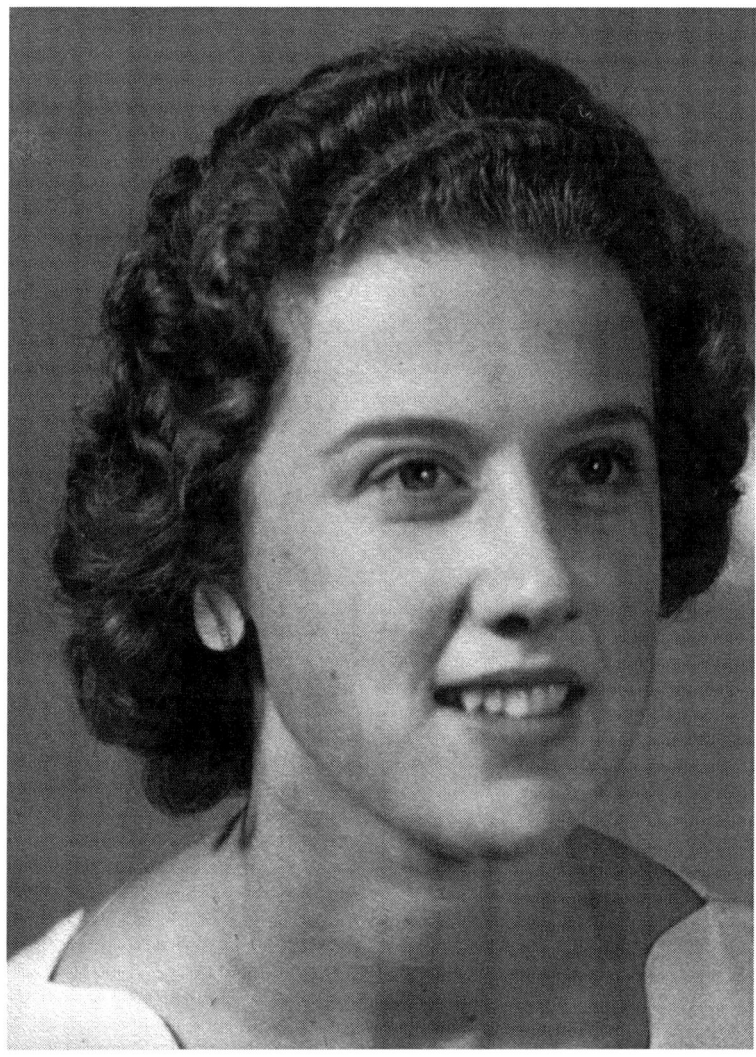

Cynthia Janice Green

He was not available and I took a message and obtained the caller's name. She was Cynthia Green from Devizes, later to become my wife and mother of our three children. I will now explain how we became married as a result of that call.

Cynthia was a clerk at the regional Driving School based in the Wiltshire Constabulary at Devizes. She had met my colleague whilst he had attended a driving course and wished to retain contact. I subsequently learnt that the friendship was not a longstanding one when I also attended a driving course some months later.

My duties as a foot patrol officer, my arrests and performance had drawn me to the attention of the Inspector when he had to nominate someone for a subsequent driving course. I was asked if I was interested in motor patrol. My first response was that I had hoped to be selected one day for CID but if that was not possible in the immediate future, then yes – I would like to be considered for motor patrol duties.

CHAPTER 4

MOTOR PATROL

As much as I enjoyed walking the beat in Falmouth, any variation on a theme is always welcome – so in due course I was sent to Devizes. Within days, an officer from the Wiltshire Constabulary on the same course informed me that a clerk in the office had seen me. Knowing that I came from Falmouth and that we had spoken on the telephone some time ago, she wondered if I would like to join her and her friend for a drink at a local public house. This I agreed and I met Cynthia Green for the first time. During the driving course we saw each other on many occasions and within six months we were engaged and later got married in June 1960.

Standard driving course Devizes 1959

I mention this at this stage as it was the telephone call whilst on guardroom duty that subsequently resulted in thirty-six years of marriage and three lovely children.

(Cynthia died in 1996 during our retirement years in Spain.)

After the driving course, which entailed much study of the law and driving procedures and miles of practical driving under pressure, I returned from Devizes to Falmouth and was immediately allocated the position as relief driver on the area patrol car. I had done well on the course, I had become a good driver and found myself a wife! The area police car, one of four in the entire county was a black Austin Westminster. It was fitted with a VHF radio and our call sign was QA4. I have the spare key ring tag to this day!

Austin Westminster Key Badge

It was a proud moment for me, a young officer, to be nominated with the position of relief driver when one of the two regular officers were on a day off. When they were both on duty, I returned to normal foot patrol. The patrol car duty was much envied by my colleagues, but they accepted that I deserved the honour, especially as in days to come, I was to instigate many arrests and deal with some major accidents whilst on patrol.

My fellow regular officers were PC May, PC Bill Fulford and PC Peter Thompson. The former became a sergeant at Saltash shortly after I joined the team, but 'Pete' Thompson and I became a regular pair on the car.

The car was kept in a garage near the police houses not far from the police station. Before each tour of duty we would make sure that the vehicle was clean and all the equipment was correct. We carried a first aid kit and a few traffic signs for use in an emergency. At that stage, we did not carry an abnormal load sign, but after I had designed and painted one that was approved for use, we were also allowed to display that

First Aid Certificate 1960

when escorting abnormal loads. When not in use, it was kept in the garage.

Our emergency warning instrument was a magnificent electric chrome bell mounted on the front bumper. We had a blue light on the roof and it was one of the first vehicles to be fitted with a loudspeaker beneath the bonnet. At the end of each tour of duty, we filled the car with petrol, washed and polished it before garaging it for the next tour of duty. We were independent of local control, but aware of local requirements. Our control was from the Force Information Room at Bodmin, manned by an inspector and team. During the day duties we may be one of three divisional cars on duty within the county. On night duty, we were often the only car within the entire peninsula and sometimes covered vast mileages in response to calls. After 2 am we seldom encountered any other vehicles on the road except lorries loaded with cauliflowers or daffodils heading up the A30 for the London markets. In the opposite direction, we would often see the film distribution van visiting the Cornish towns with the latest films on distribution. Any vehicle, other than one with a local registration ending in AF, CV, or RL was recorded and sometimes if the law allowed, stopped and checked. Our knowledge of the county with the two main roads running east to west and vice versa, gave us ample time to intercept, stop and check most suspicious vehicles. In the winter, the roads were very quiet at night and only in the early hours of the summer visitor rush westward did we see a high volume of traffic.

The divisional Traffic Department motorcyclist, PC Alfie Pittam sometimes became a relief driver on the car. Invariably this was during the winter when motorcyclists only performed duty in good weather conditions under the control of the Traffic Department at Bodmin. During my short time as relief driver, PC George Matthews also joined the relief crew. He was also interested in CID work and was a smart, precise man intent on promotion.

The divisional motorcyclist on the small BSA machine, station messenger and odd job man was a character. He was PC 'Staff' Pedlar. He was renowned for his ability to resolve most situations his way and talk his way out of trouble without difficulty. He knew everyone in Falmouth and everyone knew him! In a dire emergency Staff would appear on his machine and invite the first available officer to jump on the pillion seat and accompany him to the scene of an incident. His Corker helmet strap was never done up and sitting behind him, the pillion passenger would be lashed in the face by this strap blowing in the wind unless aware of the situation. The sight of two police officers on a small low powered motorcycle in the streets of Falmouth was common place. I never experienced it anywhere else and yet it brought immediate response and good results at low cost.

My days on the patrol car crew took me to many serious and

"QA4" A30 Lanivet 1959

also amusing incidents. One misty winter's night, Pete Thompson and I were called to Bodmin from Falmouth. The slow journey peering into the night fog was tiring on the eyes and it was almost 2 am. When we were just passing through Lanivet on the A30 suddenly, we both saw what appeared to be a figure pass before us across the road glowing as it went. "What the hell's that?" exclaimed Pete.

"Don't know," said I, "better stop and see." We had seen nothing for the past hour as the conditions were so poor, so we put on the blue light for safety purposes and pulled into the side of the road in this hollow outside Lanivet. We couldn't see anything and after a while we were about to go back to the car when the glow appeared on a tree or bush. We were somewhat apprehensive and returned to the car. The radio didn't work in the dip in the terrain and we decided that we would go on to headquarters. On the way, we tried to work out what we had witnessed and bearing in mind the location was the scene of a latter day monastery and priory of St. Bennett, our minds began to imagine everything. That time of night is not a good time to resolve problems!

When we got to HQ we told them our story. The Inspector laughed and didn't really believe us and stated that moorland people often saw things in the misty, foggy conditions. We had seen something and we needed to resolve it! On the return journey, the mist had rolled away with the dawn and nothing could be seen at the spot where we had stopped. We were still puzzled and to this day, I don't know for sure what we saw. Some say it was St. Elmo's fire, a freak condition. Others say it was a reflection of our lights in a wooded and damp area that mirrored our approach. I believe that it was a freak show of nature and weather combined. On another occasion we were called to the alleged sighting of a flying saucer over Bodmin Moor. That was soon resolved and turned out to be an helicopter from RNAS *Culdrose*. I did know of an officer who said he saw an un-identified flying object during a night shift, I never did, but was once nearly hit by a flying roof slate during a storm. I enjoyed the ever-changing weather and conditions. The full moon, the chasing clouds, the frosts, the balmy summer nights. Time to be alone and reflect on the privilege of being paid to be close to nature. Beat patrol had its compensations and so much was lost when concealed in a metal box on wheels. The introduction of the motor car was the death knell of communication of police with the public. Essential for response but did nothing for public relations. Peter Thompson was thin and wiry and enjoyed the warmth of the car heater in the winter – I preferred the fresh air and do so to this day!

On another occasion, Peter and I were on motor patrol in the Camborne/Redruth area. The local Superintendent had requested that we pay special attention to his town as residents had made complaints of excessive noise at night after the pub turned out. We had completed our patrol and our presence was sufficient to deter the troublemakers. We were going to return to Falmouth via Fraddon and once outside Redruth on the A30 in the early hours of the morning, we saw a milk float weaving its way towards us. We realised that no one delivered milk at that early hour in the middle of nowhere and decided to stop the vehicle. It was soon apparent that the driver had taken the vehicle without consent and was drunk. An arrest had to be made. We knew that the station at Redruth was closed and that Camborne may have a constable on night duty, but out of contact at that time. I arrested the driver of the float and we tossed up who would drive the patrol car and who would return the laden float to the depot. Peter lost the toss and I handcuffed the prisoner in the back of the car and took him back to Camborne Police Station that had been alerted to our arrival by the control room at Bodmin. Sometime later, a cold and unhappy Peter arrived with the float which by now was very low on battery power! After charging the offender, the owners were called and a replacement float took the milk away except that required for our much deserved cup of tea! Whilst the incident brought mirth and laughter to those who heard about it, I was contacted by Detective Sergeant Arscott some days later who in his own sarcastic way commented on our action in clearing crime for another Division! "Better you cleared up some crime for us my son," he said.

"I will," I replied – given the chance! A few days later he asked me if I was interested in detective work after a night's observation in an isolated store had resulted in the arrest of the offenders. The officer who accompanied me during that period of observation was a young probationary constable, Bill Laws. He later became a good friend of mine but sadly was killed in May 1986 whilst on motorcycle patrol duty. Later I was offered a place on a Detective Training course but before that, many other days of uniform duty followed.

CHAPTER 5

THE REST OF THE TEAM

Escorting abnormal loads took a great deal of time away from true policing duties. Being based at Falmouth we often had to collect and escort a load from the county boundary to Falmouth docks. That could sometimes take two days or more, depending on the length or weight of the load. On one occasion we got too close to a thatched cottage in a narrow stretch of the A30 and part of the guttering detached itself from the cottage and travelled with the load to Falmouth! We couldn't remove it as the ship's bronze propeller we were escorting was too high from the ground. We reported the incident to Force Control and the owner was compensated by the hauliers. Whilst the activity was a test of skill in traffic control, I was pleased to learn that in years to come this aspect of police work was handed to civilian escort teams assisted by police in dangerous and congested locations. In some areas a fee was also imposed for police assistance.

When not engaged on traffic patrol, I enjoyed the variations in tasks that came my way.

The retiring Inspector, Doug Bassett was balding! To our amazement he stated his intentions of opening a hairdressing salon upon retirement. This became a bit of a station joke which even he appreciated. Having spent hours preparing and painting decorations for the annual police ball in the drill hall, Doug Bassett asked me if I would paint a sign for his salon. He purchased a large plate glass window that was duly delivered to the police station and placed on the snooker table on the first floor. On this I was asked to paint 'Mayfair Hairdressing Salon'. This could be done in duty time I was informed! I completed the task, but in my own time and when I last visited Falmouth in the late eighties —that window with my sign writing was still in place!

The Falmouth police ball was an annual event organised by PC Garfield Slade. He was a wise man. His car and trailer would haul anything anywhere for the right price. He and his wife ran a very nice guest house near the railway station and many enquiring holidaymakers would be directed to that establishment.

Garfield was one of two older officers who did their duty in a preventative manner. Action was not foremost in their minds, but they played their part. The other officer was Percy Tamlin. Percy was a quiet man who made the most remarkable working model traction engines from machine parts. He was a very clever model maker and interesting company. Their local knowledge was priceless!

Local intelligence records were kept in the Criminal Investigation Department together with a card index of all local convicted and cautioned criminals. After a court appearance, the records were updated or amended. Access was only allowed with authority of the Sergeant – but that rule was often broken! Gathering criminal intelligence was everyone's duty. It paid dividends when crimes or mysteries were to be solved. There were no computers, only card indexes, postal communication and the telephone. All messages were recorded on form 104, Vehicle Licence enquiries were made by post on form RF 16/3 to the county where the vehicle was registered and road tax for a car in 1962 was only £5.10s per quarter! This didn't deter the forger from altering a disc after stealing one from an unattended vehicle – a very common crime!

I have not yet mentioned the ladies of the establishment at Falmouth. WPC Rosa Cox was the first when I transferred, followed by Victoria Stadden and later by Janet Curtis. All three were good at their specialist jobs of interviewing girls and

FROM			GENERAL CIRCULATION			
	Information Room, Sgt. Coombes,		DATE	T. of O.	CLASS	No.
TO	LIVERPOOL CITY POLICE - TELEX 1500 hrs. 28.5.63.					
			CIRCULATED BY			

We have had cause to examine a Ford Anglia car, 1958 model, bearing engine and chassis number 100E 569960, Reg. No. 851 ND. This vehicle was originally sold to a member of the staff of Fords at Dagenham through Fords Internal Sales Department. When they first registered the vehicle the engine and chassis number was quoted by them as 100E 556864 on the Taxation Form RF 1/1.

However according to Fords Internal Sales Records, 851 ND has the engine and chassis number as found by the Liverpool Police.

Ford Anglia bearing engine and chassis number 100E 556864 was sold on invoice no. T.58735 on 29th May, 1958, to B. L. Dale & Son, Ponsharden, Falmouth. Tel. No. PENRYN 2331.

Could you please ascertain from the above firm what Reg. No. was eventually allocated to this vehicle, also if still in your area please examine and verify the numbers.

It appears at the moment that it may only be a clerical error on the part of Fords.

Please cause enquiries to be made and ring Information Room who will in turn telex Liverpool.

RECEIVED BY		DATE		TIME

REPLY/ACTION TAKEN/CIRCULATED TO

DATE	TIME	SIGNATURE	
FOR INTERNAL USE			
COPIES OF MESSAGE TO —			
CANCELLATION		DATE	TIME
REMARKS —			

SIGNATURE............

Sample message pad

Road Fund Licence 1962

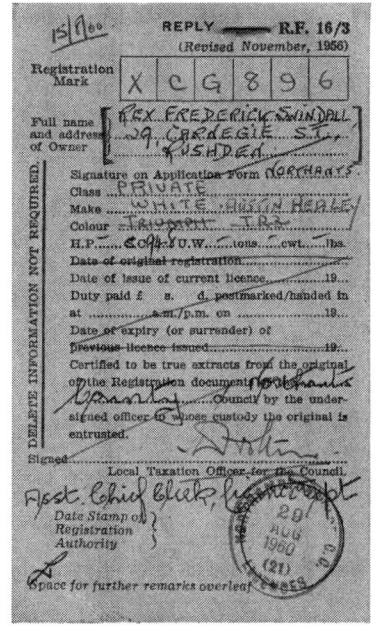

Form RF16/3

female victims. I often thought that this was the right role for the WPCs, not because they could not do other types of police work well, but that they excelled at those specialist skills. They also acted as escorts for female prisoners and were required to carry out searches of females when required.

It would be remiss of me not to mention all the others serving at the police station possibly not mentioned in an incident elsewhere with whom I enjoyed working. They were, PC Ivor Fox, PC Geoffrey Oatey, PC Brokenshire, PC 'Jock' Davidson, PC Mike Matthews, PC Lional Matthews, PC Rodgers, PC Trevor Hill, Cadet David Baber, PC Mike Rowe, PC Peter Robinson, PC John Stevens, PC Roger Doble, PC Philip Tregunna, PC Fred Rhodda, PC Tony Wilkins, PC Bill Laws, PC Trevor Hattam, PC Whatmore, PC Ward, PC Malcolm Quick, PC Dick Dawes, PC Dennis Stone and others who came and went during my time. There was also one dog handler who seemed to be around when required, although he had a divisional responsibility rather than a local role.

The station staff included one man as a civilian cleaner. He was Len Bullock, a short stocky individual who knew everything that was going on. He was the station informant!

Annual leave was taken in strict seniority order based on years of service. Only one week could be taken during the summer months. A written application on form 44 would be submitted, agreed by the Sergeant, recommended by the Inspector and approved by the Superintendent.

Detective Sergeant Arscott had promised me a Detective Training course, but I knew that I would have to wait for my dream to come true. His staff already had two regular Detective Constables, John Wilson and Donald Crabb. John was in line for promotion and Detective Constable Rodney Allen had just moved on to the Helston sub division. I just had to wait. I had impressed Norman with my interview skills during my attachment with him during the murder enquiry at

First leave application

Newquay during the latter part of July, 1958. I had only completed four years of uniformed duty as a constable and enjoyed every minute of it and to wait was no problem. I just enjoyed police work.

CHAPTER 6

THE YOUNG DETECTIVE!
HAVING A BALL!

In the meantime, Cynthia and I married in June 1960. We lived in a rented flat in Marlborough Road, Falmouth. Shortly afterwards, I was told that I was to attend the Metropolitan Police Detective Training School at Hendon in October of that same year. We were expecting our first child and I was to be away for three months. Not the best way to start married life! We also had to move accommodation as the landlady had stated that no children could live in the property. Affordable accommodation was hard to find in a seaside town where high rentals could be obtained from holidaymakers. We did manage to obtain a ground floor flat in Harriet Place overlooking Greenbank and Falmouth Harbour. We moved before Nicola was born after I returned from London. I was now a detective constable and retained the number 97.

CID course. Hendon 1960

CRIMINAL INVESTIGATION DEPARTMENT
NEW SCOTLAND YARD

This is to Certify that

Detective Constable Gordon David Stuart MADDOCK

of the Cornwall Constabulary Police Force attended a Course of Instruction at the Metropolitan Police Detective Training School, Hendon, from 3rd October to 10th December, 1960 and passed the Final Examinations in the theory and practice of Criminal Investigation.

Date 8.2.61

a/Assistant Commissioner.

A qualified detective!

After a short while, our finances dictated that we found alternative accommodation as police houses were only allocated in seniority order and we were way down the list. It could be years before we were allocated a house. We were paid an allowance in lieu of official accommodation, but that meant little in Falmouth where the landlords could demand high rents during the peak holiday season. However, in 1962 we obtained and rented a house in Tregenver Road by the rugby ground and it was our first real home. We couldn't afford proper furniture except for a table and two chairs, a double bed, a sofa and a cot. The other items I made! My first DIY in married life!

My sixteen hour days without much time off led to domestic problems and a degree of ill health on my part. Predictable meal times were few and far between and I had to ensure that I took adequate time off to be with my family. I was married to the job and not to my wife and family. With only two detective constables and a devoted detective sergeant in a town the size of Falmouth – we were stretched to the limit.

Norman Arscott was a hard taskmaster yet fair. I learned a great deal from him and his results were outstanding. He understood the criminal world and they understood him. What follows later is my indoctrination to detective work under the guiding light of my mentor, Norman Arscott. Before, I move on – there are some more interesting moments whilst in uniform!

Supt. Charley Brown reached retirement age and for his last attendance at the annual police ball, there was a special meeting in his office. It was to be a special occasion with a special buffet to match! Usually, Garfield Slade would cater for those attending with his contacts in the hotel and guesthouse business. He had the 'discount card'!

The meeting commenced in complete twilight. The office faced the front of the police station on the first floor overlooking the Western National bus station. The window was opened as Garfield's pipe smoke filled the room. The light was off as the Superintendent didn't like what he called the new fangled 'forensic' lighting. (fluorescent lighting!) He was a lovely kind-hearted man and we all wanted to give him a good send off. I was co-opted to the committee as my artistic ability meant that I would be doing the decorations!

The proposed menu was discussed. Salmon sandwiches, sausage rolls, small pasties – a must in Cornwall, and 'Hors d'oeuvre'. At that moment, Norman Arscott, who had been seconded to the meeting as an adviser, chipped in with one of his typical comments – "Horses hooves – what the 'ell do you want they things for?" (Norman had been in the Army and a chef by trade. His comments concerning food were precious!) As if to add insult to injury, Garfield suggested 'gherkins' might well add a bit of class to the menu. "We don't want none of they Gurkhas," exclaimed Charley Brown – Let's keep to good 'olsum Cornish scran! (Now I am looking for my dictionary at this stage – I thought I knew a lot about the Cornish – but now I was not so sure!)

The meeting concluded with a typical police social event style menu – all were happy and the Superintendent got a good send off at the ball.

My decorations were not too difficult to complete. I had seen plenty of potted palms and Garfield liked a lot of 'greenery' around his functions. With his trailer, he could collect any amount from the surrounding countryside. I decided on a 'wild west' theme which amused Norman. "Plenty of cowboys around here already boy," he said, "more bloody cowboys than Indians!" he added with a jovial chuckle that was his trademark.

I painted some mountain scenery on the back of rolls of linoleum that Garfield obtained from somewhere! He knew where to get anything! I had often walked along a narrow street up the hill and parallel with Arwenack Street on night duty and seen a series of carriages in an undertaker's garage. They were in wonderful condition and one looked just like a western stage coach. With a team of volunteers, I asked the undertaker, – who got plenty of business from us! – if we could borrow one or two of his carriages. They were covered in dust and cobwebs and hadn't seen the light of day for many a year. Four of us pushed and pulled these through the streets of Falmouth much to the amusement of the locals. I had the foresight to attach a poster advertising the police ball on one of the carriages – ticket sales rose almost immediately! The local police ball in the drill hall with a strict tempo band and refreshments was a posh affair and a prestigious black tie event in the town! The Mayor of the Borough, the Chief of Police and many local dignitaries attended. The application for the licence to provide liquor was always granted with a smile by the Magistrates after they had of course, received their invitation!

The events were always a great success and the clearing up

the day after fell to the early morning shift.

I think that at this stage, I should mention that there was a wind of change in the Cornwall Constabulary. Re-organisation was about to take place as with many police forces in the country. The Home Office was beginning to exert influence and that half of the police budget that came from the Exchequer had to be accounted for before being granted unquestioned as had always been the case before. Local Authorities, especially combined Police Authorities in the counties often found the money to provide a good and efficient police service. Cornwall and the Isles of Scilly authorities always met their demand and were proud of their constabulary in the fifties. The public, mostly of Cornish descent in those days, respected and supported their police. Those residents from other parts of the country that had retired to Cornwall also expressed their satisfaction of the manner in which the constabulary functioned. Life Saving was introduced on the beaches of North Cornwall and the police were very much involved. The police choir entertained many thousands of people in a county with a great tradition of male voice and ladies' choirs. Public Relations were good and a natural development from efficient policing. Only major riots had caused the need for support from outside forces, such as the fishermen's riot over the sighting of pilchard shoals along the Cornish coast and miners' strikes. Much has been written about these elsewhere.

Superintendent Brown retired and was replaced by Superintendent Tommy Walke. Inspector Basset retired and followed by Inspector Arthur Lobb. Bill Dyer, Jimmy Jackson also retired and Sergeant Ted Burgess took their place. The division was to be amalgamated with Truro and Superintendent Sydney 'Boysy' Keast was in charge. Detective Inspector Williams also headed up the new divisional CID. Norman was no longer head of the divisional CID as he had not qualified for the inspector position. Helston remained a sub-division, but we all worked to Truro. It was a big change and the beginning of Falmouth losing its status as a division. This coincided with the closure of many of the dry docks and the decline in the merchant shipping operations in and out of the port. Many ships were being tied up in the river Fal. Large tankers, roped together that rode on the tide like massive metal barriers in one of nature's most beautiful navigable rivers.

CHAPTER 7

DRINKING AND SINGING!

I remained in CID with DC Donald Crabb and Norman was our Detective Sergeant. Supt. Tommy Walke was a big-hearted man, loud yet compassionate. Inspector Arthur Lobb had been a member of the CID before promotion. He was a shiny, ruddy faced man somewhat insecure unless surrounded by men with experience. He relied on the 'books' and 'stated case' for his authority. If he liked you, it was all right – if not times could be hard! Don Crabb was a good friend and a good detective. We have remained in contact to this day. Whilst most of our working time was spent in the Falmouth town area, we also had responsibility for the ancient borough of Penryn. This too was a busy area under the command of Sergeant Dobson. Their area included such places as Deveron, Perranworthal, Flushing, Mabe, Stithians and Restronguet. The latter had a very pleasant public house owned at that time by a baker from Redruth, Mr Harvey. I often painted in the vicinity of that pub in a creek on the river Fal.

It is interesting to recall that publicans played a big part in not just providing information to a detective in those days, but also were a different breed than today and their trade was different! Whilst their licence depended on their good character, the police also were on good terms locally with most publicans. It was not unknown for the local PC to visit a pub on occasions whilst on duty and just walk through the bar and leave. This gave the officer a chance to re-assure the publican that he was aware and available should there be any trouble, but it also assisted the officer in gathering local information. There was little 'drunken driving' as locals knew that they and their vehicles had been seen at or near a pub. This acted as a deterrent. Today, uniformed police seldom visit premises unless called to deal with an incident and car parks are made larger!

Most detective officers knew all the local publicans. If criminals were meeting, then they too often chose public houses as did members of the press. Informants also used the premises. It was a centre of information in a community for all. Not all publicans were willing to exchange information and it was down to the officer to gain respect and assure that confidentiality was maintained. Most licensees welcomed the knowledge concerning persons that might lower the reputation of their establishment. It was a 'two-edged sword'!

A public house I frequented in Falmouth during the course of duty was the Four Winds at the top of Dracaena Avenue where Bill Fernie was the licensee. This was a popular pub and whilst in the main used by locals, the occasional 'dubious visitor' was soon spotted! The summer months brought many 'villains' from other parts of the country who frequented the pubs and seafront hotels. A hotel I enjoyed and visited, although somewhat isolated, was the Crag Hotel and Maenporth. The licensee was an interesting character and good company. This was one of the first hotels to offer meals as well as drinks. The trend in the late fifties was still for a public house to be a place to consume alcohol, either in a lounge bar or a public bar. The latter would be mainly for working class locals and the lounge for 'gentlemen and their ladies'. Prices of drinks as much as 'class' being the main dividing factor! Whatever the bar – they were often filled with regulars and smoke! Many more people smoked in public houses than is the case today. It was unusual for meals to be served except in a separate room set aside for the purpose. Children were never allowed in the bars – even passing through was frowned upon. A licensee was very mindful of losing his licence and the 'eyes of the law' were always on every property selling alcohol! The introduction and change of use of many pubs from their original form to 'eating houses' meant that families went to such premises in ever-increasing numbers. In the main, this was a good thing for the average family, but it also led to under age drinking by younger family members who, having discovered the habit, later returned alone or with other younger friends under eighteen to frequent the bars. Clubs were almost non-existent at that time and the disco had yet to be discovered!

A good publican was always aware of all the pitfalls and assets associated with the trade. One such pub was the 'Seven Stars' in the Moor at Falmouth. A popular place for everyone! The beer was good, the premises always clean and the locals good company. The licensee and all the Bennetts family were involved and I believe that the son, the Revd. Barrington Bennetts still runs the establishment today. I seem to remember that his sister also had a sweet shop that the younger officers frequented! I was never sure if it was her charming company or the chocolate that attracted us! Maybe both! It was well situated to observe the goings-on in the street outside, especially when raining heavily and a cup of tea was a must! When I ceased uniform duties, I often still visited both the pub and the shop whilst in the CID. The pub was a favourite location for us all as it was close to the police station and in the days before the police club, it was the recognised 'watering – hole' for CID members. It was certainly a favourite for Norman Arscott. His recommendation for that pub was what introduced me to that family.

Many other pubs in the town were frequented by merchant seamen and the licensees had to be firm and resolute in their day-to-day handling of their premises. I can't remember one publican that wasn't truly devoted to his or her trade or lost their licence through neglect or wrongdoing.

Helston also had good licensees. I have mentioned the

Harbour Hotel run by the Knight family elsewhere. There were others including the Anchor that produced its own beer – Stingo! That was powerful stuff that defeated even many a naval rating from RNAS *Culdrose*! There was one small club at Porthleven. This was run by an ex-chief petty officer and caused no trouble, although the locals were a little dubious when it first opened.

And so, working together, police and licensees produced good results. I wonder how many PCs know their local licensee today, especially in urban areas!

During my uniformed duties, I had more time off and joined the Cornwall Constabulary Male Voice Choir. This was a genuine interest of mine as I had always liked male voice choir and police band music. I had enjoyed them in the metropolitan police. The police service captured individuals with a great deal of talent. Bandsmen and singers were always to be found where there was a Celtic connection and Cornwall was no exception.

Sergeant Roy Grigg introduced me to the choir. We would travel from Falmouth to Truro on the first Monday of each

Cornwall Constabulary Male Voice Choir 1959

month. Attendance was always in your own time although the choir funds did reimburse car users for mileage travelled. Members – some sixty in all – came from all over the county and spent hours travelling to and from Truro. We met in the Truro police club, an essential institution in those days as drinking in a public place was frowned upon unless you were in the CID! The choir was conducted by Superintendent George Glover, a very talented man. He could mould the voices and produce the most exquisite harmonies. Like the Welsh, the Cornish produced some very good first and second tenors. The choir was balanced and their repertoire extensive.

The choir pianist was Chief Inspector 'Jan' Deacon. A very good accompanist if not a little heavy handed at times! He was a big, jovial man. The choir would feature special soloists, one of whom I had previously heard on the BBC *Friday Night Is Music Night* programme on BBC Radio 2 or was it long wave then? She was Cynthia Glover a wonderful colourful soprano with a very good range and selection of songs to sing. Sitting as I often did in the front row of the choir, she would stand in front of me and I felt the true resonance and emotion of her voice reaching and singing the high notes as her lilting delivery echoed through the hall. She was a wonderful soloist. There were others, male and female soloists – some from the choir itself. The entire choir was a wonderful example of public relations. The sixty or so regular members, assisted by special constables represented about one seventh of the entire strength of the Force – that was the measure of the devotion and pleasure that the choir gave to both members and audiences. There were times that the number in the choir exceeded the number in the audience – especially in remote village halls and churches. One such event remains in my memory to this day.

It was a dark, cold winter night. The choir was to meet and assemble in Lanivet parish church for a candlelight carol service. The BBC were recording the event for radio listeners over the festive season. We all arrived at the small cold and damp granite church from all four corners of Cornwall. There were more cars around the church and BBC recording lorries than anyone had seen in that village before. There was much excitement as the police choir was coming to the local church and the congregation were looking forward to the event. As we poured into the church and were seated in our four sections of the choir as required by the producer and sound recording engineer, the seats were getting few and far between. The members of the congregation were kept waiting in the cold misty air outside. The church was slowly filling to capacity, the candles were lit and there was just about enough oxygen to keep them alight! "Tis some do boy" – said a voice from near me. It was Superintendent 'Boysy' Keast. I had seen him at previous rehearsals in Truro – but this was the first time he had spoken to me, I realised then how he got his nick-name! Everyone was 'boy' or 'boysy'! This was Cornwall at its best. A packed church – packed that is with policemen with precious little room for any congregation – many of whom had to be turned away to be told the time of the broadcast as compensation for their enthusiasm and support for their church.

The recording began, the proud vicar said a prayer and the roof was lifted! The 'horgan' was 'brave' as one member remarked! The carols were by Merrit – a selection of Cornish carols that were so different to me from the ones often sung in carol services at that time of year. It was a welcome change and an experience of a lifetime. I later heard the service broadcast and remember feeling so proud that my life and time was being so fulfilled by my job and my interest in music.

My interest in music in the police service remained with me throughout my career and I still enjoy it with my art today. (In 1987, I was the chairman and organiser of the First Festival of

Police Male Voice Choirs at the Royal Albert Hall, London. One thousand members from all the police choirs in the UK took part and raised a large sum for charity. It was so essential to compensate for the strain and stress of everyday duty at all stages throughout my career. Some played sport – so did I, some made models, some kept animals – we all had to have an escape route from work. Sadly, others required alcohol to get

Royal Albert Hall – London 1987

A gift to charity – 1987

an escape from the stress of the job. In moderation it was acceptable to their bodies and minds, but to others the long-term effect took its toll in due course.

One of the finest sportsmen I met and later worked with was Brian 'Bubbles' Braybyn. He was an excellent water polo player. When Alfie Pittam moved on, Brian took on the divisional motorcycle and lived in the police house at the bottom of Quarry Hill beside the police station. He later joined the CID as a detective constable. We worked together for some time before the re-organisation. Brian had been brought up in Charlestown, a pretty little fishing village with a harbour often used by film production companies.

CHAPTER 8

CARTOONS – ALL AT SEA!

Meeting people was part of the job. If you could communicate then you gained the confidence of the residents. In those days, one was forbidden to speak to the press unless authorised. However, we often met them at the scene of an incident or in the courts. Many were veterans in the game and could be trusted. There was a Mr Spurrier of the *West Briton*. An excellent journalist. The *Western Morning News* also had a good staff with a local correspondent. The local paper was *The Falmouth Packet*. I got on well with their reporters and one, who shall be nameless, knew of my artistic ability having seen me sketching in the town on a day off. I completed a series of pen and ink sketches of various places in Falmouth and many I retained to this day.

I also had a very good sense of humour and the local paper would publish a story, sometimes with tongue in cheek to arouse local feedback. This same reporter accepted a cartoon I drew depicting the topic of the week. The editor was pleased with this novel approach and asked me if I would submit more from time to time. Now in those days, not only was liaison with the press prohibited, but a police officer was not allowed to undertake any other job or assignment. I agreed with the editor that I would only illustrate and cartoon if the artist (me) remained anonymous and received no payment for my work. This was agreed and I continued to submit cartoons until I joined the CID when I had little spare time. To this day – until now that is – no one knew the artist/cartoonist. I often overheard comments both in the police station and outside about the local 'cartoonist' in the *Falmouth Packet*. Some were

Cartoons for Falmouth Packet

good, others were interesting! That 'dangerous' commitment gave me great satisfaction!

One of the characters I used would always be found at the top of Fish Strand quay. When making a point with the Sergeant, he would be there. Often his liquor intake made him impossible to understand. He was a small man, always in a cap and trousers that were too long for him. I believe he was called Zacharia Ivey. I don't think he ever read the *Falmouth Packet* and ever realised that he had inspired a local cartoon character. Sometimes he would be accompanied by another character, Edward Galley.

When things happened in Cornwall, there was invariably a great deal of enthusiasm attached to a happening or an event. A lot was often made out of a small incident or change so it wasn't difficult to use that topic for a cartoon. (See selection of cartoons.)

During my days as a single man and whilst still in uniformed duties as a PC, I had changed my Lambretta scooter for a Morris Minor tourer. A fine blue car with maroon leather seats. That was to be my means of transport until I became a detective constable. When that day was reached, I was eligible for a car allowance. That meant that I became an essential user of a private vehicle as there were no official vehicles for use within the Criminal Investigation department. The Cornwall County Council gave you a loan spread over so many years and an amount was deducted from pay. With a mileage allowance, this meant that a new car could be purchased, so I traded in my much loved tourer and bought a Ford Prefect, pale green and brand new! This was my first new car and it also coincided with the birth of our daughter Nicola. The tourer was ideal for a single man, but very impractical for the family, especially as the prams in those days were large and by now we had a white poodle to match the pram!

We had just moved to Harriet Place and as we had no garage, I left the car at the end of the terrace on a wide pavement where many vehicles were parked. This was convenient for me as it was close by when I was called out for duty. The accommodation was expensive with magnificent views over the Greenbank Yacht Club over to Flushing and on to St. Mawes. We could see the entire harbour on a clear day from the

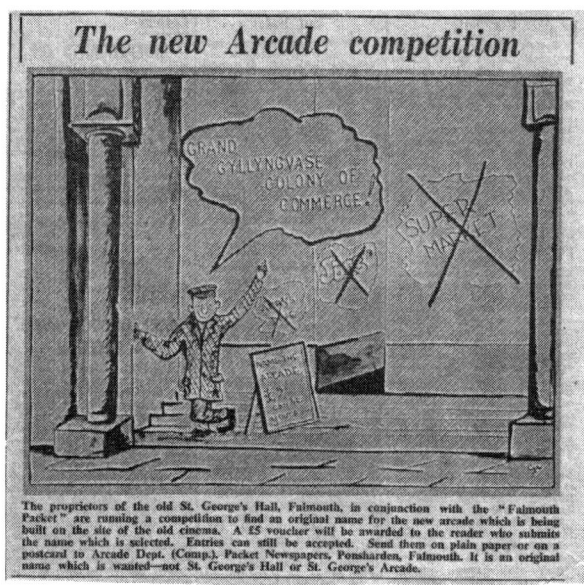

Falmouth Packet Cartoons

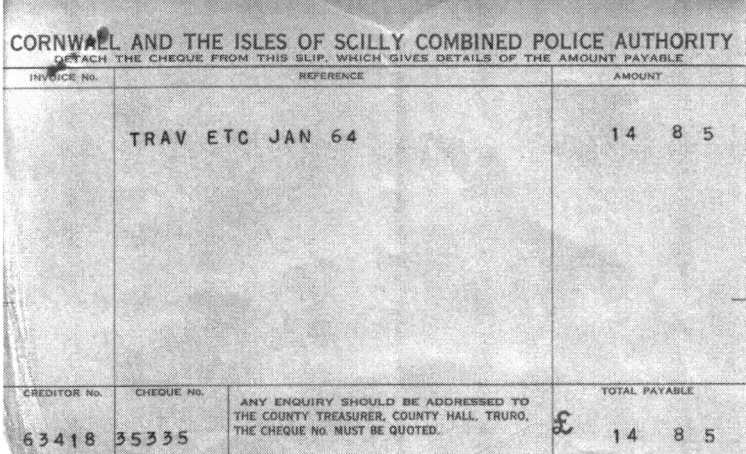

Travel claim payment form

bedroom window with all the movements of shipping and small boats. A touching occasion would be when the maroons were fired for the lifeboat crew to man the lifeboat and go to sea. It was moored offshore and you could see the crew join the boat and speed out towards Black Rock. On one such occasion there was a regatta which had commenced in calm, clear conditions but once in Falmouth Bay around Pendennis headland the weather changed and a south westerly blew up without warning. The entire station were all called out as many of the craft and crews were washed up on the beach at Gyllyngvase and Swanpool – some on the rocks. The weather could change at a moment's notice and some of the boats were badly damaged and the crews shaken.

The sea is to be respected. "Man came from Nature and if not careful – Nature will reclaim man". I learned this very soon after becoming a detective constable. Being a sea port at the western extremities of the United Kingdom, the Merchant Shipping Act entitled any sea captain to contact the first port of call to report any crime or serious incident on the high seas. We had a good liaison with the shipping agents, mainly with Fox and Co. and the Haynes Shipping line. Many of the ocean going tankers called at Falmouth for repairs and tank cleaning but others would 'steam' up the channel to discharge their cargo of oil at Fawley or further east. The police had no boat or launch and we relied upon the Harbour Master or H.M. Customs and the launch *Mongoose* to transport us to the vessel. When the ship was due to dock at Falmouth, we would head out to the shipping lanes and await the ship, board and deal with the offenders by way of arrest and interview witnesses in the crew. This was important as many crews discharged as soon as they arrived in port and it was essential to gather all the evidence whilst at sea. I carried out this duty on many occasions and on my first was accompanied by Detective Sergeant Arscott. He literally taught me the ropes! We would wait for this large tanker, some many thousands of tons, to appear out of the haze or mist and then the launch would go alongside, a rope ladder would be lowered by the crew some forty feet to sea level. The art was grabbing the ladder at the top of a swell as the launch sped to keep up with the ship. The ship would slow down but not stop as there were deadlines for berthing on a high tide at the port of arrival. This meant that if that wasn't Falmouth, you would be on board and catching a train back from Southampton! Many crimes are committed on the high seas and it matters not where it is in the world, they are dealt with at first port of call or contact. This meant that in the coming years, I was to be wallowing on a launch awaiting the arrival of ships on many occasions. I didn't mind this as I quite like the sea – that is until one trip when I was alone! With two, one can carry the briefcase and hand it to the other once on the rope ladder. Alone is another matter!

The telephone rang early in the morning and it was the Detective Sergeant. He told me that a seaman had gone berserk with a meat cleaver off the Australian coast and the Captain had locked the offender in the chain locker on the tanker. He was to be interviewed and arrested. I set out at about 5am, liaised with the Harbour Master, Captain Edwards, and two of his men were assigned to take me to the RV point about five miles out in the channel on the Harbour Master's launch. This boat was about thirty feet long, tall and had no handrails, only brass hand grips on the cabin sides, which were set about one foot in from the side of the boat. The art was holding on to one of these whilst waiting for the top of the swell, which could be about six feet, and with the other hand, grab the wet rope ladder, jump across from the launch onto the ladder and quickly climb before the ladder was dipped in the sea on the next swell! I had one of my better suits on and I had the presence of mind to tie my briefcase, with string, around my neck. That left both hands free for the tricky transfer from launch to tanker side. The huge tanker loomed up and appeared to pass for ages before the rope ladder appeared, forty or more feet of it swaying and dangling from the deck rails. It clanked against the metal hull and swung to and fro in the wind. The launch kept up with the suspended ladder and the gap closed between us and the black rusty tanker hull. I reached out with my right hand and put my right leg out to get onto one of the wooden planks forming the ladder. It was wet and my shoes would not grip, I slipped and clung onto the ladder with my right hand. My briefcase was flapping in my face and the swell came up to meet me. The launch parted company with the tanker and I got dunked in the black murky rushing water. Thankfully, I held on and put my other hand on the side rope of the ladder and hauled myself above the swell level. "Are 'e all right boy?" came a shout from the launch that by now had caught up again and I felt its reassuring presence beneath me. Had I fallen, I would have hit the launch or into the wake at the side of the tanker. Thank God I was fit and strong in those days!

I was now wet, cold and shaking from shock. I looked up and saw the remaining thirty or so rungs of the ladder that I had to climb to the deck. It seemed that half the crew had witnessed a member of the local law trying to board a moving tanker. Something that I had often done without mishap. There were a few cheers as I climbed the final rungs and one seaman helped me over the rail. He was Chinese, polite and helpful. He showed me to the bridge where I met the captain who was Indian. He seemed politely amused and offered me a change of clothing. One of his shirts, a boiler suit and slippers! Great I thought, how can I conduct a serious interview in these? Don't worry said the captain – we don't dock until tomorrow! He got the Chinese crew to clean and press my suit, shirt and my socks. My shoes were cleaned and within hours I was a respectable detective once again. I interviewed the offender who admitted the offence and was arrested and handed to the local police when we docked and escorted to Falmouth later to appear at court. I interviewed the important witnesses although the injured victim had been flown home from Australia to East

All at sea!

Anglia. Radio telephone calls were made for him to be interviewed, my train fare was arranged and a railway warrant issued for my return to Falmouth the next day. I sent a message to the Detective Sergeant with the result of the interview and asked him to inform my wife that I would be back later from Southampton the following day. I didn't mention the poor seamanship incident to anyone! It wasn't long before the crew members of the Harbour Master's launch spilt the beans! Norman Arscott made sure that I soon had another assignment at sea to ensure that I overcame my fear of the sea that came about from the incident. I realised how powerful Nature was and how Nature dictated one's fate if mistakes were made at sea. From that day I have respected the sea but the taste and feel of salt water remind me of how close I came to being possibly claimed by the sea. I enjoy sea trips and have crossed the Bay of Biscay twenty times in retirement – but no more rope ladders!

It was after conducting a similar interview on a tanker for an offence committed on the high seas off India that I had my first real curry! The Indian captain insisted that I ate with him and his parrot! This time we docked at Falmouth and not too soon. That was a 'real' curry! The offender was arrested and a witness interviewed in Norfolk. The case was dealt with at Bodmin Quarter Sessions and the police officer from Norfolk, Ronald Barham and I were to meet years later when we both transferred to the Wiltshire Constabulary as sergeants. A small world indeed!

CHAPTER 9

NO TIME FOR TEA!

Following the retirement of Inspector Bassett and his entry into the glamorous world of hairdressing, the police house adjoining the police station became empty. The ground floor was converted into the single men's lounge, the dining room became the single men's dining room and the kitchen remained the kitchen. A snooker room was on the second floor and it was decided by Superintendent Tommy Walke and others that a police club should occupy what had been bedrooms. The work was carried out by staff and contractors and we now had a very cosy bar and snooker room combined. Access was via the old front door to the house, so there was no need to enter the police station. Many good social events and Christmas draws were held there and it was a good place to find the CID after a long and tiring day. We did visit the pubs – but the quiet of the club to de-brief and in my case, enjoy a Mackeson before retiring for the night was a welcome addition to working at Falmouth. Inspector Bennet became the Inspector, an easy man to get on with and Ted Burgess, the recently arrived Sergeant and his wife became friends of ours. There wasn't much time for social life in those days, but when we did we were a 'happy family at the station' at that time.

Whilst a detective constable at Falmouth, I was investigating a case of fraud involving theft, use of cheques and false pretences. Cases had been reported all over the country, but we had many reported offences in our locality. I had circulated the male offender in the Police Gazette. A month or so later, I received a telephone call from an officer in the Garda Siochana - (Irish Police) – that similar offences had been committed in Dublin.

I was not surprised when a short while later, I received another call that they had arrested the offender. On this occasion I had the greater number of offences to be dealt with in Falmouth and other forces in other parts of UK had also sent me details of offences in their area. These would be taken into consideration in due course.

I commenced extradition proceedings at Falmouth and armed with a warrant and another Police Constable, PC Roger Doble, made plans to go to Ireland to collect our prisoner. We drove from Falmouth to Exeter and then flew to Dublin.

At Dublin airport we were met by a member of the Garda and escorted to 'The Castle' – their headquarters and prison. It was truly a prison by all standards. An imposing castle with wardens to match. Big men with large leather belts and keys! After I had gone through the legalities and exchanged documentation at the court, we were ready to escort the prisoner back to Falmouth. One snag! No flights until late the following day! We had to stay in Dublin!

We were accommodated at a local hotel and politely informed that no one visited Dublin without sampling the Guinness at source! We hadn't eaten for some time and were quite tired, but happy to accept the offer. We were taken to a golf course and club house north of Dublin by our hosts. We sampled the local brew and ate a meal. The evening came and went and soon it was well into the early hours. We had work to do the following day and escort our charge back to UK, so we requested to be taken back to our hotel. Reluctantly, we were so escorted and it was apparent that all night sessions were quite commonplace in Ireland and maybe we had failed the course! However, after a very good night's sleep, armed with the endorsed warrant we made our way to the airport with a Garda escort. Handcuffed to both of us in turn, we had special seats on the aircraft and we flew back to Exeter arriving quite late in the day. Special Branch Officers at Exeter airport made our arrival easy and I drove the prisoner handcuffed to PC Doble back to Falmouth in the back of my car. We needed a comfort stop en-route. A lay-by was all that we could find for the prisoner and mindful of an escape ploy, he remained handcuffed at that time! I often wondered what other motorists thought if they caught sight of us on that occasion! It was a plain car – my Ford – and here was a man handcuffed to a civilian in the middle of nowhere!

We arrived at Falmouth and after charging the offender were glad to place him in the cells and get some rest. Next day, the paperwork had to be completed and the first of many court appearances arranged. Then there was a remand in custody and conveyance of the prisoner back to Exeter prison to await a further committal appearance at Falmouth Magistrates' Court and subsequent trial at Quarter Sessions and eventual imprisonment.

The amount he had obtained by fraud and false pretences was quite substantial and all the effort and Irish experience made for a notable case – well concluded! This was just one of any cases I was handling at that time – unlike the TV detectives that only seem to handle one case at a time!

I worked with Norman Arscott a great deal. He was a workaholic and accepted nothing less from his staff. He was proud of the department's detection rate and the standard of their work. Having left the uniform behind, I enjoyed the freedom of movement that civilian clothing gave one, although having been in uniform duties in Falmouth for two years, I was well-known by now in civilian clothing – it made little difference. Time was forgotten in CID. No overtime, few days off and then – no payment for the extra hours worked. Most days I started at 8am and finished at midnight the earliest. Sometimes we would work through the night, take a few hours off and continue again the next day. Meals were irregular and led to me suffering from a stomach complaint. That and the lack of rest meant that I lost a great deal of weight and became very run-down. I enjoyed the work and the challenge – it was endless. There were just three of us dealing with an ever-increasing caseload and always having success. That meant more reports had to be prepared and we had to handle all our own file preparation with one typist available from 9-5 five days a week. She was excellent, Diana Mundy. She was the friend of my last girlfriend in my single days before marriage, so I knew her and we got on well. She soon married and settled down and we were all happy for her.

Norman was a stickler for having everything correct – and so it should be! We had to prepare files for the Director of Public Prosecutions and take them to London ourselves if the cases warranted such action. We had to attend the Magistrates' Court for verbal committal proceeding as everything evidential was presented to that court before it was either dealt with or sent to Quarter Sessions or Assizes to be dealt with. We would then have to re-warn witnesses, check exhibits and get the case and all involved to Bodmin or Penzance in the case of Quarter Sessions and to Bodmin for the Assize Court. Upon return, the results of the case had to be dealt with and at the same time, we had to deal with incoming crimes, interview offenders and help the uniformed officers deal with minor crimes and many juvenile offenders.

Being a member of a small department had its advantages. We all had our part to play. Norman had a tactful and cunning way of interviewing. I adopted the psychological approach and others could be the hard man or the nice man – depending on the role to be played and the nature of the offence and the character of the offenders. All admissions had to be voluntary, but well phrased questions made all the difference in the response! It was team work at its best. It was a good department and our results were respected in the county. We knew our local solicitors and barristers from 'up country' when we needed them. We knew the press, we knew the Home Office pathologists, the hospital staff and local doctors and even the Probation Service, Social Services and other agencies were all working for the betterment of law enforcement in those days. Being a port, HM Customs often assisted us and we them. Falmouth had a variety of challenges but the environment and goodwill made life easier for us all. The only thing that was suffering in retrospect was our marriage. I was missing a lot of my daughter's younger days. My wife was an excellent, devoted mother who only saw me on our occasional days off. They were few and far between.

Thankfully, Norman Arscott had his soft side and a heart of gold. He was a 'salt of the earth' character. He could be 'hard' when the occasion warranted it and on the other hand, very compassionate. He took a liking to our little baby, Nicola and called her his little 'cheel'. He often asked me, "How's my little maid my 'ansome?" As time went on and in the winter, we managed to get more time off although the daily hours were still long. Much typing, report preparation was the resulting penalty of being a successful department. We had no dictating machines although we could dictate to Diana in office hours if there was time for her to take dictation. She too was under pressure.

Everything was very methodical and precise in the administration of the station. Sgt. Roy Grigg was very accurate in his work and there was a great deal for him to do to keep the 'ship' afloat. Mileage returns, claims for expenses, transfers, accommodation, daily preparation of the 'mail bag' for divisional and force headquarters, station finances, collected fees for certificates – the list was endless. I was once asked quite rightly to justify an expenses claim upon my return from the Metropolitan Police Detective Training School. I was entitled to a rail fare to attend the course and return to Falmouth at the completion of the three months. I was also permitted to claim one return rail fare from London to Falmouth during the course at half-term. In order to make the best use of a two day break, I decided that I would purchase a single ticket from Paddington to Falmouth valid for three days. I also sent Cynthia, my wife, the money to purchase a single ticket valid for three days from Falmouth to Paddington. (This was the same price as a three day return ticket in those days.) As my parents resided in Tiverton, east Devon, about halfway between London and Falmouth we both travelled one day and met at Exeter. The following day, we exchanged tickets and returned to London and Falmouth respectively from Exeter. The only 'offence' that we committed being the transfer of a non-transferable ticket according to the railway bye-laws.

When I submitted my claim for a return fare as entitled, Sgt. Roy Grigg saw me and asked me if I had made the return journey as he had tried to contact me in Falmouth about another administrative matter during the weekend in question. He thought that I was claiming for a journey that hadn't been made. I explained to him what had taken place. He thought it through and although realising that I hadn't put in a fictitious claim, I had bent the rules slightly! He understood the reason and thought that I could be reimbursed but would have to clear it with Supt. Walke. I duly repeated my tale to the Superintendent who was sympathetic with my motive of trying to make the most of available time. As there was no difference in the amount claimed to my entitlement – I was duly refunded the fare.

Our income in those days wasn't that great. Every legitimate expense made had to re-claimed quickly to balance the monthly budget. CID work was hard on the pocket and expensive. The allowances didn't cover the expenditure on petrol, meals and purchase of drinks for informants. We had no official informants' fund and any monies for that cause came from our own pockets. Although we had an allowance for

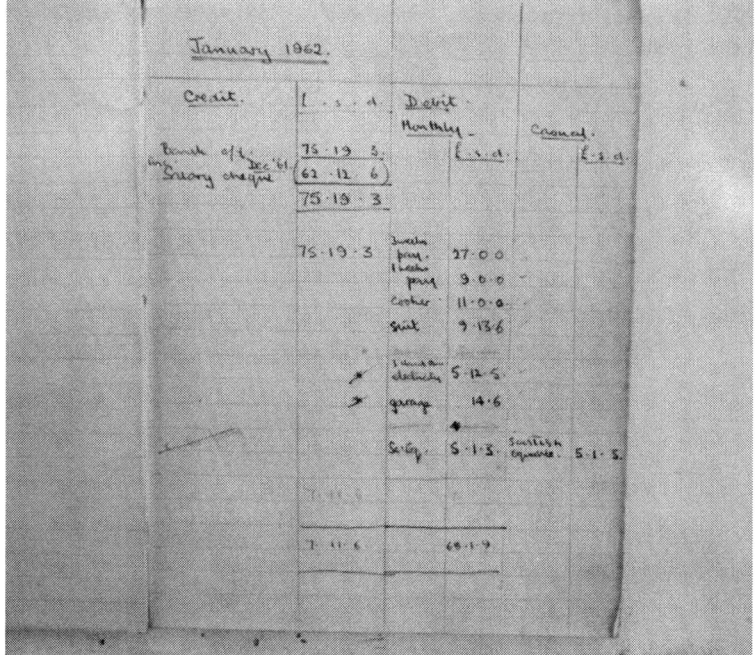

Household accounts 1962

mileage on police duty, that barely covered the cost of petrol and oil. The vehicle still had to be maintained and serviced at our expense. Yes – we had a vehicle on a cheap ' hire purchase' type loan from the County Treasurer – but the monthly deductions meant a reduction in monies paid into our bank accounts for day-to-day expenditure.

I opened my first bank account at Lloyds Bank in the Moor, Falmouth with £20! Our monthly income in 1960 was £54 paid by cheque. (£.s.d in those days, there being 20 shillings to the £ and 12 pence to the shilling.) We had a long tin box at home divided into sections. One for the electricity, one for the gas, one for the rent, one for a mail order club, one for petrol and the final section – our family pocket money and £5 a month for my expenses on duty! By 1962, my pay had risen to

£62.12s.6d per month as a detective constable. Our rent was £9 per week, a second-hand electric cooker cost £9, a new suit for me cost £9.13.6d, our monthly electricity bill was £5.12s.5d and a service for the car cost 14s.6d – police rates! We managed to save £5.1s.3d. each month with Scottish Equitable in the hope that one day we would be able to afford a mortgage and our own house! My only other income was a monthly refund for using my own car – (essential car user as a detective officer) – this refunded me on average £14 per month. We lived on a simple diet of cheap foods and many a day we had reheated leftovers from the previous day! I had no time for gardening then so I couldn't grow my own vegetables. Many uniformed PCs had wonderful gardens and allotments. Garfield Slade always had a surplus at a reasonable rate and brought many things to the station to be sold to his colleagues! Uniform duties had their assets – Criminal Investigation had its rewards and greater job satisfaction for me.

I did achieve a bit of boat building in the kitchen! I bought some marine ply from a boat builder and a boat building magazine. With the use of borrowed cramps, I cut and glued together a nine foot pram dinghy. I made the entire boat with inner floorboards and oars with a mounting board on the stern for an outboard motor. I purchased a Seagull 4 HP petrol engine in a marine sale and my craft was ready to launch! One snag! I had built it in the kitchen, varnished it with marine varnish and it looked a "proper job" to all who saw it and commented on my work – but how did I get it out and how did I get it to the water? By turning it on its side and sliding it on rollers, I managed to get it into the garden. It was too good to put in the water – it looked 'ansom', gleaming there in the sun. A trailer was needed, but I couldn't afford one! Only one solution, buy two wheels and make one! This I did and made a trailer out of wood. It contravened the Construction and Use Regulations as my 'springs' were not in accordance with the

Pandora Inn – River Fal

regulations for the weight being carried. OK, I thought, I will call it a launching trailer – that made it legal! No one stopped me when I was using the car and trailer and the boat as I did have a repeater number plate with lights! I didn't need brakes as the trailer's unladen weight didn't require me to fit them!

Sgt. Jackson had just retired and before he went, he approved of my progress from rod and line beach 'fishun' to 'proper 'fishun' from my boat! I only chugged around the harbour, launching the craft from the old RAF Air Sea Rescue base at the end of Arwenack Street. I caught very few fish, but enjoyed the trips over to Flushing and up the river to Penryn. I never ventured out of the inner harbour as I was no match for the vast tankers being pushed and pulled by harbour tugs and the turbulent propeller wash they created in their wake.

I did take the outfit to the Helford river and visited Durgan on many occasions. We enjoyed the Ferryboat Inn. There I could launch from the beach whilst my wife and Nicola awaited my return with the 'catch of the day'! On many occasions this

Ferry Boat Inn – Helford river

was no more than a few mackerel or crabs which fancied my lure or bait. Often they waited a long time for my return as the 4 HP motor was fine going out with the flow from Durgan to the sea and mouth of the river, but unless I awaited the change of tide, the motor just about made headway against the current and it took ages to return to Durgan. On one occasion, I had to get ashore and wait for the tide to return up river. So much for my boating days! I kept the boat for a season until one day someone who wanted a tender for their yacht offered me a price I couldn't refuse – so I sold it there and then with the motor. We needed the money and I wasn't getting the time to use the boat as often as I would like. When I did take a day off – it invariably rained – as it often does in SW Cornwall – and I couldn't go fishing and enjoy it.

CHAPTER 10

THE CIRCUS COMES TO TOWN!

I tried to make the most of time off and when I could I would negotiate with the other DC and vice versa for cover so that we could both plan to do something we wanted to do. I had chosen a day shift as there was a visit to Newquay that week by Bertram Mills circus. This in itself was a big day for Cornwall! Much advertising and excitement. I asked someone in Newquay CID to get me tickets so that my wife, Nicola and I could go to the circus. The tickets were obtained and I was looking forward to that evening. I told my wife that all she had to do was get something to eat for her and the baby and pick me up at the police station at 4pm: Norman Arscott had agreed that I could get away early! (I had started at 7am that day having been called out early to investigate a break-in at a beach café.) Normally, we would work 8am to finishing at about 6 pm on a good day – often that would be 10pm or later! The following day we would work 9am to midnight. This was a regular routine as each evening at 10 pm, the train arriving at Falmouth carried that day's publication of the Police Gazette which was entrusted to the guard. The train had to be met and the document collected. That ensured the latest wanted list and list of serious crimes being available that same day. On this day, I was intending to finish work at 4 pm to meet my wife at the police station.

I had been making enquiries in the town area and at 3 pm called into the Red Geranium café – a favourite watering hole for the constabulary. The ladies there looked after the officers requirements for tea and cakes or saffron cake with cream if you were lucky! I sat in the café in the corner facing the door, a procedure most policemen adopt so they can see who enters the room. (I find it difficult to this day to break that habit!) I was having my tea and cake when a youngish Pakistani, smartly dressed came and sat at my table. He was carrying a holdall. He ordered tea and placed the holdall on the floor. It was obvious that he was a merchant seaman as I could see his name was on the bag with his merchant seaman's number! We said nothing and when I had finished eating, he said to me "Hey Johnny, do you want to buy a watch?" Now – that phrase alone almost made me laugh as it was the type of thing you hear in plays and at training school. I replied that I might – depending on what he had for sale. He bent down and unzipped the bag which was full of watches! I couldn't believe my eyes. What a coincidence and what a scoop. On the other hand – what bad luck for me on the only day in months that I had promised my wife a trip to the circus. I decided that I had to act. I told the man that I had my car in the car park and my money was in my wallet in a jacket pocket. Why don't we walk to the car park and do a deal there? So I paid for my tea and cake and we left the café together much to the astonishment of the ladies. I didn't make my arrest there and then as I had learned that such decisions, made at the wrong moment, can cause additional problems, although I had my suspicions and sufficient evidence to act – I delayed the arrest. When I got to the car park, which was opposite the police station I told the man that I was arresting him. He couldn't believe his bad luck – the first person he tries to sell a watch to was a policeman!

Once in the station, the bag was emptied and the contraband listed. There were many watches, some smelling of crude oil. The offender explained that he had hidden them in plastic containers suspended on black cotton inside the huge holding tanks on his ship and later sewn them into a waistcoat to avoid detection by HM Customs officers during their search of the vessel. When the customs men had searched the ship – they were not found. Norman Arscott was in the station and agreed to explain to my wife, who by now was waiting for me, what had happened. I was engaged in the investigation and for continuity sake, I was now committed to charging the man once HM Customs had been called and the value placed on the property. I had arrested a modern day smuggler! The offender was convicted and fined the following day at the Magistrates' Court having been kept in custody overnight. Because few would believe the story – I kept the newspaper cutting of the case to this day.

Smuggling case report

My wife went to the circus on her own – we were both disappointed, but this was a good example of 'a policeman's lot not always being a happy one' – even with good intentions at the beginning of the day.

There were many occasions where plans were made and cancelled. Friends understood why we couldn't commit ourselves to appointments for social occasions. Those with less understanding of our work, often thought that I was making excuses for not being able to attend functions, concerts and family events.

I suppose that Norman instilled in me the work ethic I adopted. The commitment was however a natural one as no one gave up their line of enquiry until all aspects had been exhausted. With no mobile phones, no radios – everything took time and because of that – no stone was left unturned – investigations and elimination of suspects led in the end to evidence to pinpoint the offender. The methodology of crime investigation in those days left nothing to the programming of a computer to work it out for you. Your instinct, your 'gut feeling', patience and devotion led to results. We shared our intelligence, we knew the suspects from their history, antecedents and 'modus operandi' and together with their whereabouts from recorded sightings and lifestyles – policing was a committed art form. I am not sure that it is today. As with many other professions, the service commitment of the mid-twentieth century has been replaced with an hourly paid job description where there is little scope for common sense and initiative. I accept that other factors have changed – society itself has changed, cost effectiveness and the strive for efficiency through the political overlords dictates policy today more so than the time I am describing. What has been lost has been lost forever – the devotion and for many – service factor. What is the right or wrong priority? Law enforcement or capitulation to change! Only time will tell.

CHAPTER 11

MURDER AND ACCIDENTAL DEATHS

However, we worked as a team regardless of politics and our aim was to detect offenders for reported criminal offences. Our priorities did exist. The detection of offences against the person took precedence over offences against property. Indictable offences took priority over misdemeanours. The uniformed officers played the major role in preventing crime by their mere visible presence in public. If on foot and in communication this gleaned information which was fed into the system and assisted the detective.

If a major crime was committed such as a murder, the Headquarters CID under Detective Superintendent Sydney Norman Roberts and his bag carrier, Detective Sergeant Freddie Cornwall, would appear on the scene. Detective Superintendent Roberts was a tall well-built Cornishman, a typical Sherlock Holmes style detective. He always wore his brown trilby hat and tweed jacketed suit with highly polished brown shoes. He always smoked a pipe and glowered as he spoke.

In mid July 1958 an elderly man had visited an isolated toilet block during the day at the Headland, Newquay. Newquay at that time was a crowded summer holiday resort. He had been murdered by a person who hit him over the head with a large stone. The motive appeared to be robbery. Norman Arscott and I were seconded to Newquay to assist in the enquiry. This was my first major murder enquiry and the sort of incident that I had read about and had motivated me to join the police when I had read the work of Bernard Spilsbury, the Home Office pathologist. We assembled at Newquay police station with other detectives seconded in from Liskeard, St. Austell and Truro. We had to work quickly as the only clue was that someone had seen a man wearing a green shirt near the scene of the crime. Holidaymakers would be leaving Newquay at the weekend and making enquiries by contacting other forces where they lived by telephone or letter would be time consuming and costly. The more people we could interview in Newquay's hotels, guest houses and bed and breakfast establishments as soon as possible – the better. Questionnaires were prepared and an incident room set up. Card indices were commenced and tasks allocated. This was the forerunner of a Major Incident procedure that was soon adopted by most forces. House to house enquiries were made by uniformed officers suitably briefed for their task. It poured with rain and whilst this kept people in their holiday accommodation, officers got soaked in one of the wettest summers on record for the north Cornish coast!

A few days into the enquiry, the changeover of holidaymakers had taken place, there was no trace of 'green shirt' and it was apparent that there was little or no forensic evidence to assist. The Chief Constable decided that in keeping with Home Office guidance in those days, a force could call upon the expertise of the Metropolitan Police to assist in murder enquiries. Such a request was made and a detective superintendent and a detective sergeant duly presented themselves at Newquay railway station for collection. I collected them and took them to their hotel. Within hours they had decided that the local police station was no place for their briefings and de-briefings – they were to be held in the hotel bar! This improved morale in the late evening when they produced what only the Metropolitan Police could – £100 for incidental unquestioned expenses from a black attaché case. Time proved that this amount was capable of being topped-up from week to week and the hotel bar was the main beneficiary.

Everyone worked hard. When not allocated a specific task, I accompanied Norman Arscott, – the Detective Sergeant with all the local knowledge – as he knew Newquay well. We searched every beach hut night after night, disturbing many a courting couple as we went. We picked up one or two on the wanted list for petty offences in other parts of the county – but no sign of 'green shirt'. Had he been in Newquay – he would have been found. After about a month of endless hours of investigation, little sleep and hours of daily travelling to and from Newquay from Falmouth we were returned exhausted to our 'normal' local duties. The remaining detective constable had worked hard in our absence with some aides to the department but our local detection rate had suffered in our absence. It was a good introduction into CID work for me as I had been an aide to the department for this enquiry.

'Green Shirt' was never found, the officers from London enjoyed their Cornish break from 'the smoke', their expense allowances were well spent and they returned to London. Detective Superintendent Roberts and a small team continued follow-up enquiries for many months but the case remains undetected to this day. Even after his retirement, Detective Superintendent Roberts would visit the scene of the crime in the hope that the offender might return. Often the offender would return to the scene of a crime, but on this occasion, he never did.

Local events kept us busy with a degree of variety in their format. Each and every suspicious sudden death had to be investigated by a member of the CID when reported, and there were plenty of them. Hardly a day went by when we would not find ourselves caught up in a tragic death, a cot death of a baby, a suicide, a fatal accident at a place of work or in the home or just an unexplained death in a public place. Traffic accidents were the exception unless there was evidence of manslaughter. The traffic patrol officers dealt with all fatal accidents on the roads. This part of our responsibility needed courage and a sense of humour, good liaison and understanding with the medical profession and the ability to apportion genuine sympathy to those in families who had lost a loved one. Our liaison with the coroner was very important as it was he or she that decided the cause of death that could alter the entire investigation. Most deaths were explained from the circumstances, history of the deceased or from the results of a post-mortem. I didn't mind attending post-mortem examinations as I had 'A' level zoology qualifications and had dissected animals and found the anatomy interesting. It was another art form and it brought the Michelangelo out in me. I always was interested in how the body worked and more so – why it fails.

We had been called to a dry dock in Falmouth docks where a hulk of a vessel was in a dry dock for hull repairs. It had a crew mainly from Pakistan. One crew member had been ashore and apparently missed the gangplank from the dockside and fallen to his death to the floor of the pumped out dock below the gangplank. There were no witnesses. We carried our own home-made scenes of crime kits in those days. Dusting powder, brushes, exhibit tubes and bags and a fingerprint roller, ink and pad. For any serious event or crime, we had to call upon one of two scene of crime officers based in Bodmin. Other divisions also called upon their services so there was often a time wait at a scene before assistance of the expert arrived. We couldn't afford cameras and if we could, they were large wooden plate cameras, complete with tripod and black cloth. Not the sort of equipment you needed every day. We did have an old well-used camera with tripod fixed to the floor at the correct focal length so that even the least experienced officer could take a reasonable photograph of a prisoner face on and from the side. Complete of course, with the mandatory chalked name and date of birth board in focus beneath the portrait. Surprising as

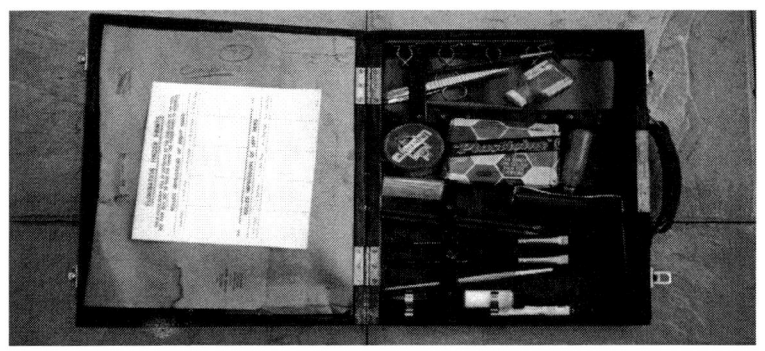

*Homemade
scenes of
crime kit*

it may seem, many photographs were still taken with the black
cloth over the lens and with large photoflash bulbs that failed
to illuminate. These were soon replaced by our own photo
floods at Falmouth with better results.

On this occasion we waited for some time before we were all
lowered to the bottom of the dry dock in a huge metal bucket
from a dockside crane! There was myself, Frank Laity, the
headquarters Scenes of Crime officer and PC 'Staff' Pedlar, the
local despatch rider who had been first to attend the scene,
corker helmeted with flaps a-flying!

He had a wicked sense of humour. Here was this poor
foreigner, miles from home that had met his end by falling into
a dry dock. It appeared from what we had found out whilst we
were waiting, and later confirmed by the pathologist, that the
man had consumed large quantities of alcohol before returning
to the docks.

Photographs were taken, there was no visible sign of foul play and the body had to be placed in the large bucket to get it to the dockside to await the funeral director. (They were called on a strict rota and details kept in a register at the station to avoid claims of unfair trade allocation!) Before the body was moved all official photographs had been taken on my instructions and I was to prepare a report for HM coroner in due course that day when PC Pedlar had obtained all the statements. Before D.C. Laity left, Staff Pedlar, the clown that he was on many occasions, insisted on one last photograph of him with a foot lightly placed on the body as if with some 'trophy'. I was not for this, but Staff was Staff and the photograph taken. We got back to the dockside and I asked DC Laity to send me the photographs for my report as soon as possible as the shipping agent had to arrange with the funeral director for the disposal of the body after the coroner had opened the inquest.

I completed my report that day and the following day had to attend a court in Penzance. Without informing me, the photographs had been sent to Falmouth by traffic car from Bodmin. As I had already submitted the report to the duty uniformed Sergeant, it had already been submitted to Inspector Lobb. When the photographs arrived, the Sergeant didn't look at them but passed them to the Inspector to go with the file to the coroner.

The following day, I was summoned to the Inspector's office. Quite rightly, Inspector Lobb, a puritan and serious minded man had not taken kindly to the inclusion of the photograph requested by Staff Pedlar. Had I seen the photographs first, I would have removed it and given it to PC Pedlar. Now it was too late and I felt ashamed that I had been a party to such an irreverent act.

I spoke to DC Laity and warned him of what had happened as Inspector Lobb was going to report the matter to

Headquarters so that DC Laity could be repremanded as I had been. PC Staff Pedlar was seen by Inspector Lobb and somehow survived the incident. All I can add being that at the bottom of that dry dock, as I explained to Inspector Lobb, the body and the irreverent act could not be seen by anyone from above as the body had fallen and bounced off the stepped dock wall to a final position beneath the giant hull of the vessel. Nevertheless, I felt rather ashamed of the incident and tell it only because we all had to take the rough with the smooth and accept when we had been wrong or part of a wrongful act. It was normal to have a sense of humour when dealing with some tragic incidents as without one – many would fall apart and break down.

Ironically, Staff Pedlar was involved in another incident involving a body which will come later on in my career. This time, his initiative saved the day!

CHAPTER 12

MERRY CHRISTMAS!

Dealing with dead bodies became part and parcel of a detective's life. Because of the small department, they were frequent events and came when not always welcomed. It was Boxing Day, 1961 and having been on call on Christmas Day, I was to have the day off. Like many days off – they never arrived! Just before I was about to enjoy my lunch at home, the telephone rang and the uniform Sergeant – Sergeant Roberts informed me that an elderly lady had been found dead in an isolated house at Swanpool, just behind the lake. I went to the scene and it was the house of a recluse, it stank and reeked of cats' excreta and urine. The body had been there for some time and as with many elderly people they die and their passing went unnoticed for days. I was happy that whilst a sudden and unnatural death it would be explained away at the post-mortem. I spoke to Dr. Hocking, the Home Office pathologist whom I knew quite well and who lived at St. Ives. He was going to attend as soon as possible – just get the body to the mortuary and he would be on his way. This I arranged and with the local PC, awaited the arrival of Dr. Hocking. He arrived about one hour later accompanied by his wife who was also a doctor and assisted him with post-mortems. "Bit of raw deal this," he said. "Never mind, we were about to have our lunch – we've brought it with us!" With that and in company of the deceased on the slab, his good wife produced a neatly packed hamper from the rear of the car parked outside and brought it into the mortuary. "Fancy a turkey sandwich, officer?" she said kindly. "We can't eat all these dear," she retorted to her husband as he pulled on his rubber gloves. By this time my

View from Swanpool looking east

appetite had gone, the stench of the body was enough to turn any hardened PM viewer. I felt all right, but a turkey sandwich – No! "Very kind of you doctor," I said, "but I think I will wait until I get home for any food – I don't fancy one now."

"Come on," she said, munching on an overfilled sandwich, "let's get started on this ol' dear, this won't take us long." Within minutes the dissections had taken place between mouths full of Boxing Day fare and their hamper was empty! I was assured that the death was due to age and a heart attack – natural causes. No need for an investigation, just a job for the uniformed officer to locate relatives and file a sudden death report.

I returned home later that afternoon still reeking of the stench of death. That was one of the most difficult odours to get rid of. It remained in the nostrils for hours and was often repeated many times during my career. I didn't eat much that day, drank a bit to try and celebrate what was left of Christmas and from then on – turkey sandwiches have never been one of my favourite snacks!

When it came to cunning detective work and taking short-cuts to bypass officialdom, Norman Arscott was a past master. Early one morning, about 3 am the phone rang and Norman, with whom I was now quite friendly as I conformed to his stereotyped detective requirements, wanted me to meet him at the dock gates. "Can't tell 'e over the phone what 'tis about – see 'e there 'dreckly'." This was a Cornish phrase I heard used a lot. It meant as soon as possible to most but has a variable time scale of response to suit the occasion. It's a bit like mañana is to the Spanish!

It was a cold, misty morning. I had passed no one from home to the docks. They didn't start work until 7 am. This I knew only too well as I had once almost caused a riot by stopping half a dozen dock workers in my uniformed days for failing to stop on their cycles at a dangerous 'Halt' sign on their way to work. Some were prosecuted – but they respected me from then on. (How could I condone dangerous cycling in those days?) Norman was at the dock gates before me with two men whom I recognised as customs' officers. We went into the dock and boarded the *Mongoose*, the customs' launch normally moored off Town Quay. We headed out to sea and on the way Norman explained to me that he had received a telephone call from Sweden that two men were gunrunning weapons to Africa. The boat, a converted MTB (motor torpedo boat) type of vessel, was due to call at Falmouth for provisions and water – bunkering – in nautical language. It was known from the Swedish police that the weapons had been stolen from a warehouse in Stockholm. We were not far off Black Rock, a marked beacon at the entrance to the river Fal when we heard the engines of another boat in the fog. We stopped engines and wallowed on the morning tide and swell. Not a very pleasant experience when you haven't had time for breakfast! The engines started again and the vessel headed towards us. "Don't start up yet," said Norman, "let the buggers fall into our trap!". The dark shape of a sleek boat could just be seen heading towards Falmouth. No lights, no radio communication was heard. "Now give them time to tie up as it gets light and we will make a routine stop and search. You boys had better do that – we will wait," said Norman. We crept in at a slow pace, the mist lifted and the vessel tied up alongside the quay. No flag of identity or condition flag flying as should have been the case. They had come from a foreign port and should have identified that fact. This was enough for the customs, with far more powers than the police, to act. They boarded and a thorough search was conducted. "No firearms," one whispered to Norman and I who were in the cabin on the customs' launch. "They've bloody got them," grumbled Norman. After a long interview in perfect English – well apart from Norman's Cornish – it was decided that after a caution for not displaying correct identity, they would be cleared by Immigration Officers that had now arrived, allowed to take food and water on board and leave immediately. It was now well into the morning and I was starving! We had a few biscuits and coffee and waited for the boat to leave. "Don't follow too close when they go – hang back – tell them they are free to go and wish them a good trip," said Norman. That was done and they looked pleased and headed out to sea. We followed slowly and only within binocular viewing distance. The shipping lanes to Falmouth were busy and by now crowded with sailing boats, yachts, pleasure boats and large tanker and merchant vessels on the move. It was easy to take cover amidst all the moving vessels. The launch stopped. "That's it," said Norman. "What are they up to?" We waited and after a few minutes they continued out to sea. "Follow them we must," shouted Norman. "How fast will this tub go?" (An insult to the customs men!) That spurred them into action, the engines revved to maximum limit, the stern sank back in the water and the bow rose as the wake appeared behind us. An exhilarating ride followed as we closed on the Swedish vessel. "Stop!" commanded the customs officer on the loudspeaker, and they did. Jumping aboard it was apparent that the two occupants were looking concerned and guilty. They were wet and the floor of the boat was wet. A further search revealed the weapons – consisting of dozens of rifles contained in polythene-type material bags – roped together in the fore-cabin compartment. "You're under arrest" said Norman, "back to Falmouth." We later learned that the weapons had been left suspended in the waterproof containers beneath a Trinity House buoy where they had stopped before entering harbour. On the return trip, they had stopped to recover them!

Back at Falmouth we unloaded the vessel, took all documents and the two men were arrested and conveyed to the police station in a taxi with the weapons.

What followed amazes me to this day. Det. Sgt. Arscott telephoned Sweden and spoke directly to the Chief of Police in Stockholm. Only Norman could demand that! He told them that the men and the weapons were at Falmouth police station. In theory, courts, embassies and consulates and headquarters should have been involved by now and talk of such things as extradition to the fore! Not for Norman. He said he was going to persuade the two men to return to Sweden if they would go voluntarily. After many promises and almost threats of what would happen to them if they didn't agree, they agreed to the suggestion. Police officers were to fly from Sweden to Heathrow and book return tickets for the two offenders. The two would be taken to Heathrow and with the help of the then airport police, taken to the plane by their 'escorts' and handed over to the Swedish officers on the plane. After a talk on the phone with someone I didn't know, the plan was amended and Det. Sgt Arscott went to Heathrow and picked up the two

Swedish police officers, brought them to Falmouth and they returned with their two offenders in a taxi. The weapons were shipped back later when someone came to collect them and the boat after liaison with the customs. Somewhere along the line, I am sure they should have appeared before a UK court – however all parties seemed content with the result of dealing with the arrest of foreign nationals the Arscott method!

This was an example of practical policing that couldn't be carried out today.

CHAPTER 13

VISITING OFFENDERS

I learned a great deal from Norman Arscott. I accompanied him on many investigations and also carried out a large number on my own. Murders were many for a country area and a few investigations I was involved in are worthy of mention. Manslaughter, domestic murders, rapes, sexual assaults and assaults were commonplace wherever one served – Falmouth was no exception.

Sergeant Ted Burgess had replaced Sgt. Jimmy Jackson and we got on well. He was a good artist and more of a 'training' man than a practical policemen, but he was kind and considerate, as was his wife, Mandy. We all became good friends. During my time on CID we would assist and train PCs in the art of crime investigation. A woman had called at the station complaining of being raped. There were many such allegations made by prostitutes who failed to get paid, so we had to be certain that the allegation was genuine. We didn't hound the prostitutes, but knew who they were and the taxi drivers would confirm their clients and places from where they worked. Only if there was a complaint would we act and enforce the law. None solicited in the street, they used the public houses frequented by the merchant seamen, mainly those near the dock gates. We would often visit one of the pubs after collecting the Police Gazette from the nearby railway station. As it was a terminal station, carriages were often searched in sidings at night for wanted criminals and the 'work place' of the prostitutes. As the docks declined in repair work, so did the trade for the prostitutes and they gradually left town. Our complainant that evening had in fact been raped and from a description given by the victim, Sgt. Burgess and I were able to draw a likeness of the assailant. This resulted in a detection when someone recognised the likeness to a known criminal in Penryn. We had many photographic albums of convicted criminals, used frequently for identity parades from photographs when it was impossible to find twelve similar people for the 'line-up'. They were paid a shilling each for their trouble when we did ask the Inspector to arrange a 'parade'. Identikit had just been introduced in larger urban police areas, but Cornwall was yet to introduce the system for the compilation of a likeness to the wanted persons. Ted Burgess and I also drew pictures of stolen antiques and other items that had to be included in a 'dealers' circular'. After every crime when property was stolen, we circulated the details to dealers in the area. On many occasions, the honest dealer would tell us who had brought the property in for sale. Some kept detailed books of names, (often fictitious names!) or a description of the vendor. Much of the petty crime was committed by 'locals' – many from the 'Old Hill' area of the town or from the new council estates at Penryn. Many were recidivists or juveniles.

Sometimes a wanted criminal would visit the town, especially if he had once been in the merchant navy. One night I had made an enquiry at the hospital and decided to walk back to the station by a 'short-cut' through a housing estate. I saw a man coming towards me with a holdall. I stopped him and told his that I was a police officer and that I wanted to know what he was doing late at night in that area. I asked his name and he said, "Terrance Alwyn Jones." I asked to look in the bag and he dropped it and ran off. I was fit, but he was too quick for me so I decided to return to the station and check the name given with New Scotland Yard. The procedure was to telephone the 'Back Hall Inspector' on Whitehall 1212, give your number, rank and name and he would telephone you back. A simple security system as he would only telephone known police station direct line numbers. He told me the man was wanted for many burglaries all over the country and gave me a Police Gazette reference.

I told Detective Sergeant Arscott that we had a wanted burglar on 'our patch' and he mobilised the rest of the staff. It was now well into the early hours and the town was quiet, so anyone on the move should be detected quite easily. By daybreak Jones was still at large. The dog handler, traffic crews and most 'off duty' personnel joined the hunt. I felt guilty that I had failed to arrest the man before he ran off, however I stayed up all night and continued the search the following day. PC Whetter, like most older and mature constables knew the territory well and thought deeply about where to search. He decided to walk the railway line from Penryn to Falmouth as it passed near the rear of the position where I had last seen the man. Mid morning, PC Whetter saw the man asleep beside the track in a tunnel. He was arrested and we handed him over to a northern force that had circulated him. Not all criminals were local and during the summer months, many travelling criminals visited the town, cars were stolen, worthless cheques were tendered. (No credit cards then!) and accommodation was rented and deserted during the night without payment. Cafes were broken into and shoplifting was on the increase. The retail trading methods had just begun to change. Before there was a counter between the purchaser or would be thief and the owner and staff. Now, retailers were placing goods where they could be taken. The retail trade was to blame for the temptation put in the way of the thief. Crime Prevention advice was often given, but insurance and an allowance on the part of the retail trade to build in losses from shoplifting did little to deter offenders. When someone was caught, they were handed to the police and that made more work for an already stretched force. There were no private security companies in Falmouth or Penryn – only in the big cities 'up country'! Summer was never 'quiet' – the same establishment had to deal with the thousands of holidaymakers and the crime that accompanied them as during winter months. That establishment was based on the requirement in the winter months, the local population – so many per head to one PC. That was the cross a west country force had to bear!

We were now living in Tregenver Road, Falmouth. Our next door neighbour, Mrs Maynard, ran a 'Bed and Breakfast' establishment. I returned from work one evening and was unable to park my car outside our house. I remembered the registered number of the vehicle blocking my front door and parked my car around the back of our premises. I had just sat down, exhausted from a long day, eaten a meal when the front door bell went. Mrs Maynard was excited and upset. A lodger had left without paying about half an hour before. I could see that the car had gone and I had the number. I telephoned the police at Launceston as I had a hunch that the offender would leave the county and there was only one main road, the A30 eastwards. Two hours later, I received a call that the car had been stopped and the couple detained. I arranged for them to be held overnight and went with a WPC to Launceston the following day and brought them back to Falmouth They were charged with obtaining credit by fraud under the then Larceny Act, as they had done the same thing throughout the summer on a number of occasions all over the country. I circulated them as being in custody and requested a remand in custody as they were of no fixed abode. This was granted and by the end of the week's remand, I had a list of almost one hundred other offences to be taken into consideration, including obtaining petrol without payment and petty theft. They were found guilty and sent to the Quarter Sessions for sentence as the man had a string of previous convictions. We had to fingerprint and photograph our own prisoners, send the details to New Scotland Yard and the South Western Criminal Office at Bristol and in return would get their criminal record and a result of case form to complete later. This way, criminal records were later updated in force, having been certified by the court, and copies returned to regional and national Criminal Record offices. After committal, either for sentence or trial, the file with all the evidence had to be typed by the court and passed to the higher court with the collated evidence of all the other offences to be taken into consideration. On this occasion, these pleaded guilty, so witnesses didn't have to be warned. I did charge them with two other offences, but the remainder were taken into consideration when they were sentenced. Even with a guilty plea, I had to attend Quarter Sessions for the case and others in the court list to read the antecedents of the offenders. These had to be compiled and verified with letters to ex-employers etc. All time consuming office work on top of the practical aspects of the job. The calendar soon filled with commitments that could not be avoided. Preparation for and subsequent court appearances took up a lot of time.

CHAPTER 14

MURDER –
A HANGING OFFENCE IN 1963

Whenever a foreign national came to live or work in the area, we had to register them as aliens. They would complete a form if they could read and understand English, submit it with two photographs and five shillings. The application was processed at force headquarters and the certificate returned to the division for delivery to the applicant. This ensured that their residence was correct or that they were working as stated. With a growing hotel trade, the number of Spanish and eastern European applicants also grew. This was a real tie and made life ever more difficult. The caseload was increasing daily, we were getting exhausted as the summer wore on and we longed for the winter months. We seldom saw a beach or had a day off – that was for the holidaymakers only!

Detective Sergeant Arscott

DC Brian Brabyn was my final 'workmate' in an ever changing station and department before I was transferred to Helston. We got on well and being of similar age we shared the caseload well. Before, I often felt that being the newest and younger member of the department, I took more than my fair share of the work. I was a willing horse and enjoyed the work!

It was during a morning when we were inundated with a whole

host of new work, that the phone rang and we were told that a farmer had been murdered at Constantine within our division. This was a small country village at the head of the Helford river near Gweek. Normally, nothing happened in Constantine and the PC stationed there had little to do other than issue cattle movement licences, deal with theft of farm equipment and animals and keep the local population happy. He and his wife would live, eat and sleep the job. This was commonplace and accepted by officers in a rural location on their own. He had a bicycle or small cc motorcycle as transport and the wife was as capable in most cases of dealing with matters as her husband. No one logged hours worked, they were there when required and trusted to put in an average of about forty-two hours a week. It was their patch and they were proud of it and respected for it. Even their days off were flexible to confuse the local villains and often not taken. If they did take a day off the phone would be answered and the message diverted to the divisional or sub-division if urgent response was required. In most cases, the matter would wait until the next day.

Detective Sergeant Arscott said we should toss up for who accompanied him on the murder enquiry. HQ staff would also be involved later, but I lost and Norman and Brian Braybyn went to Constantine. They met the pathologist and I stayed in the station to set up the Incident Room and get additional staff organised. Once at the scene they reported back that the farmer had been badly attacked with a sharp instrument. The farmhouse had been ransacked and the motive looked like robbery. Farmer Rowe lived alone and there were no witnesses and it appeared that the attack had taken place during the previous night. Pathological evidence later proved this to be the case from the temperature of the body when found. A farmhand had discovered the body when starting work the following morning. From local enquiries, Norman had established that previous employees had included one with a local criminal record. He told Brian Brabyn and he set off to look for this man. In the meantime, equipment was required at the scene. Plastic or cellophane bags were used in those days and were required urgently. I was to obtain some and take them to the scene. The headquarters Scenes of Crime officer was on his way. I obtained the bags from the hospital on the way to Constantine and I was allowed into the farmyard that had been cordoned off. Not that it was necessary as there was no one else about and it was in an isolated location. The press had not got wind of the incident yet. Only after the introduction of police radios some years later did the press mysteriously appear at the scene of a crime at the same time as the police! At this time, they were informed when the time was right or if publicity was required to assist the police.

The farmyard was a typical yard, animal and cow dung everywhere and chickens running around and the farmyard cats. Norman asked me if I had the bags. I had as instructed. He told me that there were some fingers or a finger that had been amputated during the attack to the deceased farmer's head. It appeared that the farmer had placed his hand on his head in an attempt to protect himself from the attack. "Mark the place and protect the evidence or place the bit in a bag."

"Right," I said, "where is it?"

"Over there," he said pointing to an open space! I went but couldn't see anything resembling part of human anatomy, only muck and dirt. "It's not here," I said.

"Got to be, you must be blind," came the reply. The part was never found but the farmyard cat was noted to be licking its lips and walking away from the scene! I never forgot from that moment the importance of immediate preservation of all evidence at the scene of a crime. The body was marked, photographed and removed and the inquiry went into full swing. I returned to the station to hold the fort and deal with all the daily crime that was still being reported.

Two days after the initial report, the Chief Constable decided to enlist the help of the Metropolitan Police Murder Squad as the Cornwall Constabulary Criminal Investigation Department was stretched to its limits. Detective Superintendent Maurice Osborne and Det. Sgt McPhee duly arrived at the local railway station in bowler hats, overcoats and with that little black bag with the money for incidental expenses. This was going to be Newquay all over again!

I had set up the Incident Room, everything was being indexed and recorded. Statements were taken and tasks allocated, completed and returned. Nothing materialised and at a daily briefing, the Metropolitan officers were bragging how 'they' would soon be clearing this one up and returning to London. "Like 'ell," said Norman and muttered some other inaudible words that no one heard. Later that day, Norman was nowhere to be found. Where had he gone? We were not concerned and he was quite capable of handling himself in times of trouble and he often did his own thing. That was Norman!

I was in the office at the station after the evening de-briefing and we decided to adjourn to the bar for a night cap before calling it a day. When we got there – Norman was there with a grin on his face. "Where have you been?" we said. Putting his finger to his lips he said, "tell e later." The Metropolitan officers had gone to their hotel for dinner and an early night after the debriefing knowing that there had been no developments in the enquiry that evening. "When we were alone, Norman said, "E's in the cell boys."

"Who is?" we asked. "The bugger that done that farmer in – Pascoe." We were then told that Norman had arrested the man Russell Pascoe on suspicion of another offence and the duty sergeant had accepted the charge on the understanding that things would be completed the following morning. No one was to mention "suspected murder"!

The following morning, two bright and breezy London

detectives came into the station and informed us that they would be making progress soon. We sat down to the morning's briefing and tasks were allocated, but nothing was mentioned about Pascoe. Just as the session was about to end, Detective Superintendent Osborne asked if there were any questions. Norman piped up having been silent until then. "He's down in the cells – he done it – I'll go and interview him – coming?" The two London detectives looked at each other. "Can you explain Sgt?" Norman did!

It appeared that Pascoe had worked at the farm and was about to join a boat at Gweek. He had done so, but the boat returned and Norman had waited at the small quay at the head of the Helford river for the return. Pascoe appeared and Norman arrested him for stealing something from the farm which only Norman knew at that time was missing. It was often the case that a small unimportant item would be retained by a thief and lead to the detection of an offence.

Pascoe admitted the offence and was charged with murder. He implicated an accomplice, Dennis Whitty who was also a thief from the area. He lived in a caravan at Perranworthal. His caravan was searched by me and we found hundreds of cigarettes between the lining of the walls. His girlfriend was also arrested but later released. The murder weapon, a large knife, was never found having been thrown into the river at Deveron on the road to Truro. Whitty was also charged with murder and they appeared for committal proceeding at Penryn Magistrates' Court.

It emerged that both men had conspired to fake a helicopter crash in a field at the farm. They were wearing crash helmets like flying helmets when they awoke the farmer, Mr Rowe and attacked him and cut and beat him to death. Money concealed in a tin in a piano had been stolen and items from the farmhouse. The piano had been broken up during the course of the crime.

Both then appeared at Bodmin Assize Court and were sentenced to hang for their crime. That hanging was the last double hanging to take place at Bristol and Winchester Prisons on 17th December 1963.

During the course of the committal and Assize Court hearings, I often spoke to Whitty who knew he would hang for murder. His girlfriend and he had intended getting married and I often gave her a lift – (as she was a witness) – to the Assize Court at Bodmin. She asked what would happen to him – I never said! She must have known that this was a crime that didn't pay!

CHAPTER 15

HELSTON QUAINT OLD CORNISH TOWN!

There were many other interesting and amusing incidents whilst I was doing duty at Falmouth, but my time to move on had come and I was selected to be posted to Helston. At this time, Falmouth was reduced to sub-divisional and a Chief Inspector Station under Chief Inspector Gerry Tremelling. Det Sgt. Norman Arscott remained in the CID with Brian Brabyn and Trevor Hattam who replaced me as a detective constable.

Helston was a lovely Cornish town famous and renowned for its Furry Dance, or Flora Dance. It was a sub-division within the Truro Division as was Falmouth at that time. I was to replace DC Rodney Allen who had been promoted.

The Inspector in charge of the sub-division was Jack Dunn. A smart gentleman with a welcoming manner. I had not met him before, but we soon got to know each other well as I was the only detective officer for the entire Lizard Peninsula and had direct access to the Inspector on many matters. Sgt. Len Oatey and Sgt. Allan Tilley were the two uniformed Sergeants. One lived in the house adjoining the granite police station and

Helston Police Station

we were to live in our first police house at the other end of the building. It was 1963, we had been married three years and now had our first 'free' accommodation and a house at that! We moved in and were very happy. My wife was expecting our second child. We both liked the location and the town and its people. For the first time we had a front garden for flowers and a detached vegetable garden at the rear behind the Inspector's house and station yard. We also had a small safe courtyard for Nicola to play in.

Len Oatey moved on to headquarters. That was a pity as we were in the choir together and got on well. We did meet up again when we both transferred to the Wiltshire Constabulary, he as an inspector and me as a detective sergeant – more of that later! Alan Tilley was a Londoner who had joined the Cornwall Constabulary after leaving the Royal Navy. He and his wife were good friends of ours. Len Oatey was replaced by Sergeant

Sherlock!

George Cowling and later by my good friend, Ted Burgess from Falmouth. We were getting to know the other members of the force and they were getting to know us. I felt an accepted and proven member of the constabulary. I still attended choir practices and concerts and I returned to one of my favourite sports, small bore rifle shooting.

Helston Police Station had been modernised and I had a large light office on the first floor to the rear of the premises. Mary Hoskins was the typist that I shared with the Inspector. She had an adjoining office at the front of the station across the top of the stairs from the Inspector's office. Beneath her was the enquiry office and on the opposite side of the ground floor – the Sergeant's office. At the rear of the enquiry office there was a storeroom and two cells and a small exercise yard. The entire building, including the two houses was built of granite. A typical grey example of Cornish architecture as adopted by the Constabulary. Many police stations throughout the county looked similar.

My Ford Prefect was worn out so I exchanged it for a Morris Mini Traveller on the county grant scheme. I was to cover a great deal of ground in the peninsula and needed a practical and economical vehicle with two rear doors for exhibits, prams and now – garden equipment! I borrowed a cultivator and started on the garden. It was lovely soil, loam, and well manured by a local farmer. I built chicken houses and kept fowls. The eggs were marvellous and their droppings were placed in a large cauldron with added rain water for liquid plant feed. The produce in the warm Gulf Stream climate of The Lizard grew without any difficulty. I enjoyed country living and we lived a pleasant and relaxed domestic life for the first time. Work was intense, but I was alone and could manage the caseload and work whenever I pleased around the clock. As long as I was there, the Inspector knew that I would always be available and reliable when wanted. I once again lived the job and was still married to detective work. When the sergeants wanted to share the night duty call by putting the night phone through to a house between midnight and 8 am I took my share and they appreciated that as we worked as a team.

The uniformed officers were a selection of mature officers with one or two younger ones. There were many sections and country stations in the sub-division, each with a married constable and family living on the job in a village. Mullion, the Lizard, St. Keverne, Ashton, Rame and Porthleven – all were country stations. Other officers lived in Helston in police houses about ten minutes from the station or accommodation in the town itself. My friend Bill Laws transferred from Falmouth and together with PC Dick Osborne, PC Doug Wesson, PC Bill Pankhurst, PC Mike Matthews, PC Bret Harvey and PC Peter Robinson – the team was complete. (Others, whose names I have forgotten – came and went during my stay at Helston.)

CORNISH FLORA DANCE
TIME FOR TEA!

Cynthia, Fiona, Nicola and Cha-Cha

We were given a small sum of money to purchase paint and wallpaper for the police house and that soon became a cosy home. We added more furniture and bought more beds for parents and guests. We were living a normal family life at last. The poodle 'Cha Cha' moved with us and settled in well. My dahlia blooms in the front garden were admired by passers-by in the summer and the good old Cornish daffodils filled the beds in the spring. The house had no central heating, only coal fires in each room. If not lit in winter, the damp, misty weather from the Atlantic can soon be felt and condensation appears on the cold granite walls. The weather was always mild and the rains heavy when they fell.

Our meat provision came direct from the local slaughter house, we had our own eggs and vegetables, milk was delivered and we wanted for nothing. In my spare time I continued my studies for the promotions examinations that I could soon sit as my five years was up – I had been in Cornwall that long! I sat both examinations at County Hall Truro. I passed the

FUZZY MEMORIES   109

Educational Examination to the requirement for the rank of inspector and the police subject – general duties, crime, traffic and administration to qualify me for the rank of sergeant. Not only did I pass the latter examinations, but so had 70% of the establishment of the Cornwall Constabulary. Promotion to sergeant was not by interview board, but by qualification, ability and selection on recommendation. I knew it would be a long time before I would be considered as I had met many capable and intelligent men and women in the force during my time with them. I was prepared to wait as I enjoyed the work that I was performing as a detective, especially as I was now alone in a rural sub-division. Norman Arscott still kept an eye on me as we were in the same Truro Division and I would consult him when the need arose. He would often pay me a visit if in the area and see his little 'chil' – now almost three years old. My main boss was Detective Inspector John Williams. He seldom contacted me and left me to organise myself and liaise with Inspector Dunn. If the latter was happy, Truro were happy! I knew Detective Constable Ken Pinder at Truro and my liaison with them was good. Superintendent Keast, a choir member was our divisional boss. He knew me and that made life easier as well.

My daily routine would be repetitive unless I was called out earlier, I would be in the office at 8.30am. The country station officers would tell me about any crime in their areas that may want my assistance. Normally, I dealt with the serious crime and that within the borough of Helston. Many officers were competent and very capable of investigating petty crime to a successful conclusion. When an arrest was made, I even taught them how to photograph and fingerprint their own prisoners and fill in the appropriate forms when I was not available. They enjoyed being involved to that degree. I would liaise with the Inspector and Sergeant at 9am and we would plan our day. Maybe even take a half day off – something that I couldn't do in Falmouth. I was sometimes called back to Falmouth for court cases arising from my earlier work there. As time went on – the frequency diminished and I spent all my time in the Helston sub-division.

As fate would have it, I was in Falmouth attending court, when my wife realised that the birth of our second child was imminent. I was there all day and when the time came for her to be taken to hospital – I was not there! Thankfully, Sergeant George Cowling came to the rescue and conveyed her to hospital at Barncoose, Redruth. All children were born at that hospital, about ten miles from Helston. Upon my return to Helston, I telephoned and went to the hospital too late to witness the new arrival but pleased that Cynthia had given birth to another daughter, Fiona. On the way, I stopped and bought some daffodils from a group of gypsies that I knew at Carn Brea – everywhere else was closed and they came to my rescue. I built up a good relationship with the various gypsies in the peninsula and by using tact and good humour – they too often gave me useful information in return. If not hounded, they were interesting groups of people and often, little trouble. The daffodils, almost a bucket full – were a standing joke for a long time and the staff at the hospital first thought that George Cowling was the father – until that is, I eventually arrived! We were a 'family' station at Helston, always helping each other and sharing daily events. Cynthia made good friends of many of the wives for the first time and they had children of similar ages to Nicola. We could also obtain babysitters readily that meant we could enjoy some time together and go out for meals and social occasions.

Our babysitters in the first year came from the Royal Naval Air Station at Culdrose just outside Helston. I had a very good liaison with the Commanding Officer and the Master at Arms, Bill Nurse. A number of offences were unfortunately committed by RN personnel when they were 'ashore'. With the co-operation and the powers of naval discipline – they were soon apprehended and dealt with either by the C.O. or ourselves. On many occasions, the most severe punishment and deterrent was handed out by the C.O! The Chief Wren welfare was a wonderful lady, it was her responsibility to look after domestic welfare and the welfare of the WRNS on the station. If we need a babysitter – she would find one or even two! I would collect them from the station and return them after my wife and I had enjoyed a welcome break and an evening out. I must admit that many of the young ladies selected were very attractive! They would spend a great deal of their 'down time' on the beaches topping up their tans and being young and trendy. When 'off duty' they would not fail to attract the eyes of any gentleman! I remember one evening I collected the babysitter, she was a tall tanned blonde, a beautiful girl with a personality to match. I conveyed her to our home and whilst we were out, my wife said, "There's no way you are taking *her* back to the camp alone tonight – I will do it! I had no intention of being other than the perfect gentleman I was – but agreed to the return transport being provided by my wife. On the next occasion we wanted a babysitter, my wife undertook both transportation duties and direct liaison with the Chief Wren Welfare!

All our babysitters were lovely attractive ladies, not least one who became a family friend to this day. She is Wendy Bate, at one time Wendy Laws née Pascoe who later was married to my best friend in those days, PC Bill Laws. Sadly he was killed in a motorcycle accident whilst on duty in May 1986. A tragic loss to Wendy and the Cornwall Constabulary. Wendy married again later on and still resides in Cornwall. She has a true, homely Cornish personality. The bathroom window of the police house adjacent to the police station at Helston where we lived was at the front. Whilst shaving in the morning, I would hear the 'clippity clop' of Wendy's high heeled shoes on the pavement as she walked past from her home to Boots the chemist where she worked. We exchanged waves and if we didn't see each other – one of us was late for work! She was my alarm clock and our babysitter for many years, Nicola was now four and Fiona a baby. Both are 'Cornish pixies' and because they were born when we lived in Helston have the

Wendy – the babysitter with Bill and May Pankhurst

traditional right to dance in the midday Helston Furry Dance. More about that later!

Cornish pasties are all part of living in Cornwall. My wife was taught how to make pasties by a Cornish lady, Joyce Oatey, wife of Len Oatey who I mentioned earlier. I love pasties to this day! Ironically, it was my wife, a 'Wiltshire Girl' who taught Wendy how to make pasties and many other practical household things. Nicola was Wendy's flower girl at her wedding to Bill – a lovely Cornish wedding at Helston. The church or chapel in Cornwall, whether Weslian or Methodist, was always full in those days and an important part of rural life. Helston had a very 'tight' community, a very loyal and supportive population and as the only Detective Constable, I was known to them and they to me. I was for the first time in my police career, a real and accepted part of the community.

We knew the doctors, the vicar, the ministers, the magistrates, the headmasters, the publicans and the implications of the inter-related families. The Gilberts, the Pascoes, the Wearnes, the Hendys and all those other Cornish names, that were all part of Helston. I was a 'foreigner' – yet knowing that – they still accepted me – I was now one of them. You couldn't force yourself upon a Cornish community!

The police station was on the route of the great May celebration of the Flora, Faddy or Furry Dance. The quaint old Cornish town came to a standstill. This ceremony, repeated throughout the day on four occasions between 7am and 5pm – of pagan origin – drove out the evil spirits of winter and brought the tourists in! It also brought with it my big annual headache! Criminals from 'up country' would descend on the town. Pickpockets, daytime burglars who took advantage of people being out of their houses at certain times coincidental with the dances, car thieves – the lot! My crime complaint book was always filled on the nearest Saturday to the 8th of May. We had assistance from other police stations with officers drafted in for the day and I had support with other plain clothes officers seconded to me to assist. The members of the Special Constabulary also played a big part in crowd and traffic control. It was a busy day – 6am to 2am on the following

All together in the Flora Dance!

FUZZY MEMORIES

Helston Town Band

Sunday morning. Many offences were detected later when the criminals left town and were stopped leaving the county. The peninsula had its strategical assets.

The main dance of the day, at midday, is danced in top hat and tails with the ladies beautifully attired in long colourful dresses. For the band, it is the third dance of the day having commenced their first commitment at 7am and again at 10.15 am for children and those not entitled to dance at 12 noon. The last dance is at 5pm. In and out of the houses they dance, the bass drum beating above all other instruments. Crowds wave and clap in the narrow streets and invariably the sun shines. It was a happy day, despite the additional crime that was left for me to detect.

Knowing of our duties in the town, some criminals would also take advantage of our commitment and for example, force open explosive stores at quarries and turn to the vulnerable villages around Helston whose occupants had 'come to town' for the day.

I couldn't get away from complete involvement with the adjoining Falmouth sub-division and we would assist each other with 'borderline' cases. Norman Arscott contacted me one day and wanted my assistance to interview two elderly ladies that had lived with an elderly gentleman in a bungalow at Rame, a location on the sub-division's boundary. The gentleman had died under suspicious circumstances and the post-mortem had confirmed the presence of a poison in his body. We interviewed the ladies who eventually admitted that they had put weedkiller in home-made jams that had been fed to the deceased. The jams we seized contained matching chemicals to the organs removed from the deceased and the forensic laboratory at Bristol provided the conclusive evidence. This case was the first that reminded me of my original interest in the work of Bernard Spilsbury and the use of science in the detection of crime. I had achieved my ambition, science had proved the crime. Both ladies were committed for trial and convicted for their part in the crime.

On another occasion, Norman telephoned me and asked if I would accompany him on another investigation as a 'refer to drawer' cheque had been passed to someone in my sub-division. This had been drawn to his attention by the Metropolitan Police who had detained a young man in London for tendering other cheques from the same cheque book. (If in a series, one assumed that there was an intent to defraud, rather than a mistaken assumption that funds were sufficient to meet the tendered cheques, and therefore possibly a civil debt.)

I met Norman at Deveron on the way to Truro. He had the address of a large country house that I didn't know existed. The gates were of large wrought iron and impressive. We were permitted access by a gardener and ushered to the front door of the house which was answered by a butler. After the presentation of our credentials, we were shown into a sitting room filled with precious antiques of foreign origin – possibly

French. The chairs were dainty and looked too fragile to sit on. Norman was a big man! I suggested that maybe we should sit on the larger upholstered chairs. This we were permitted to do by the butler. I had been told by Norman beforehand that he wanted me to accompany him as I was "the bright boy from up-country" and this person was "special"! (Norman was the kindest man you could wish to meet, but he was very conscious of the fact that he had left school and home at a very early age and without – as he would say – 'heducashun'. Because I spoke with only a slight Devon accent and 'could write proper' – he always saw me as brighter than he was. This I doubted as Norman was very 'streetwise' and no fool!) However, we waited and a very elegant lady in her late fifties entered the room. Norman started the conversation, "Mam – your boy up in London 'ave been a bad boy!"

"Oh officer – what has he done?" came the reply.

"Well 'tis like this see – he been writing cheques on a stolen cheque book – we think he may have stolen it from you."

The lady replied, "I did throw my old book away when I closed the account in London – is that the one?"

"Could be," said Norman. At this point, I entered the conversation and hinted that if the funds were forthcoming and the victims reimbursed, it could assist the son in his predicament. Although he had committed a crime on this occasion with his criminal intentions, meeting his debts may placate the victims. He had admitted what he had done and the Metropolitan Police could consider cautioning him as he had no previous convictions. Whilst there would be no guarantee that this would be the case, we could report that it was being handled within the family and leave the final decision to the Metropolitan Police. The lady agreed to pay from another account and arranged there and then for her solicitor to contact the Metropolitan Police when this had been done.

It was at this stage that the lady revealed her true identity.

She was a princess in exile from Luxemburg! We had not been told this by the Metropolitan Police as the son had not informed them of his mother's status. All we knew was that someone important lived at that address and almost as a recluse behind those iron gates.

Before we left, the lady asked if we would like to take tea with her. This we agreed and were shown around rooms on the ground floor and gave advice regarding security, which seemed almost non-existent. This was appreciated.

We were left in the dining room and seated at a small table. Tea was duly served in the finest bone china cups I have ever seen. The porcelain translucence was to be seen to be believed. They were real antiques, hundreds of years old! They were duly filled from an equally beautiful teapot. Milk was offered and accepted and added to our tea. The cups were small and so different to the large mugs that policemen often handled. Norman was impressed. He looked at his empty cup, lifted it towards the light from the window and exclaimed, "Luvly cups you got 'ere mother!" I could have dropped through the floor! Here we were with a member of another country's royal family and she was being addressed as 'mother'.

"Thank you Sergeant," she said, "do come again sometime and I do hope my son won't bother you again."

When we got outside the gates, Norman looked at me and said laughing as he often did, "Did I say something not proper?" I explained as he wanted me to and from that day on Norman always told that story against himself – that was the sort of man he was until his death in 2001. "You clever buggers from up-country – we'm all the same down 'ere," was one of his favourite sayings.

I was very fond of Norman John Arscott, the lad who had left school early, joined the army, served at the Normandy landings and survived, trained as a chef and joined the Cornwall Constabulary and been a police constable on the edge of

Bodmin Moor at a village called Blisland. He had passed his sergeant's examinations and become a good detective sergeant of the 'old school'. He never took advantage of a wrongdoer, he was firm and kind and his heart was in the right place. I learned a lot of practical policing from him and his teachings assisted me when I was on my own at Helston. My success was due to him being my mentor. He was what the Cornwall Constabulary was all about – 'all for one and one for all'.

CHAPTER 17

TIES WITH THE PAST!

Old ladies, lovely old country estates frozen in a time warp were to be part of my life once again when I was called one evening to a mansion near Manaccan in the Lizard Peninsula. I had received a telephone call from a maid that her mistresses wished my personal attendance. They had read my name in the local paper and wanted to see me. I knew not why until I arrived at about 7.30pm. I was greeted by the maid who showed me into a dark hallway which lead to a dining room. Fully dressed for dinner were two elderly ladies all in black. "Please do come in," they said in unison. "We want to report that a man we employed has left with some of our silver." This had taken place some days earlier and like many people of that generation, they were reluctant to inform the police immediately in case the items had been misplaced.

Having obtained the details, I found that my complainants were two sisters and direct descendants of the famous author Quiller-Couch. Their lifestyle was still captured in decades past.

I circulated the details of the wanted man who had been engaged by the ladies and he was arrested for a similar offence in the north of England. He was the typical fraudster and conman that sought employment with the landed gentry and the like to perpetrate crime. Thankfully, the property was eventually recovered and the offence was taken into consideration. The two ladies had never left their mansion for years and had not visited Helston for some time. It would have been difficult to get them to leave Manaccan to give their evidence before a court.

On my days off, I would visit the outlying beauty spots to sketch or paint. Manaccan was a favourite place for me as I had been there when on holiday in Cornwall in the mid fifties. My girlfriend at that time had a grandmother, Mrs Oates, who lived in a wonderful Cornish cottage with stable door and roses adorning the walls to the slated roof. The church had a fig tree growing from the tower wall and the hamlet was situated at the head of the Helford river, not far from Gweek. The tree-lined hollows

Showing the way in Cornwall

down to the green waters of the river were damp and lush. Lily of the valley grew wild and water loving birds frequented the many inlets at high tide. That was another privilege of being a detective in such a pretty part of Cornwall.

My routine daily crime detection resulted in many court appearances and getting to know the magistrates, especially their chairman. One evening, I was out patrolling alone in my own car looking for a burglar who had been breaking into shops in the town. I had seen no one and had an outstanding invitation to visit the Chief Petty Officer's Mess at RNAS, Culdrose, so decided to visit the base. It was now about 11pm and as the pubs were shut and we had no police club at Helston, I could get a 'night cap' at the mess that were permitted to have different hours as allowed by the CO. I had a good liaison with the regulating staff and an open invitation to visit the mess. In fact, I became an honorary member.

As I left the restricted area travelling towards the station, I saw a man pushing a wheelbarrow. Now, it doesn't take Sherlock Holmes to realise that few people garden or build in the dark at 11pm. There were no houses in the vicinity and nothing but a long pavement alongside the road. I drove past the man, turned around and faced him in the car headlights. He stopped and I could see that he had been drinking as he dropped the wheelbarrow and as he did so, it tipped and the contents tipped on to the grass verge by the pavement. There was no one else about at that time, so I quickly turned the car around again to face the right way at night and stopped once again. I walked back to the man and saw him collecting things from the pavement and placing them back in the barrow. I thought at first they were eels or fish as some shone in the reflection of my rear lights. To my amazement, when I shone my torch on the contents – they were ties – hundreds of them! I told the man who I was and because of his drunken condition, I had no problem in offering him a lift to RNAS Culdrose. He doubtless thought he was going back to his bunk and a good night's sleep! The camp was only a few hundred yards up the road and I quickly transported the seaman to the guardroom, told the Regulating Staff (RN Police) and MOD Police to detain him whilst I went back for the barrow and contents. I retrieved all the ties and the barrow and with it sticking out of the back of my new mini estate – (how useful it had become!) – I returned to the guardroom. I decided that I would now arrest the seaman formally and take him to the police station. The Sergeant came out to join me and rather than spend the night in his bunk – that seaman spent the night in the police cell at the station. The snag now was, there was no one on duty at the station – it was well after midnight! The Sergeant called in the night duty constable and I went to bed. The irony of this arrest was that it was our turn to prepare the prisoner's meals. We took it in turns living next to the station. Either the Sergeant's wife or mine prepared prisoners' meals and were reimbursed for our trouble. (The prisoner often got my meal when I was late home and I made do with something else!)

The following day, paperwork having been completed by me early in the morning, the man appeared before the magistrates. The problem then arose, the shop that had been broken into was a gentlemen's outfitters owned by the chairman of the bench! This was duly noted by the court who continued with the chairman standing down, but still on the bench! The man pleaded 'guilty' – what else could he do! The case made headlines in the paper, the ties were returned and that Christmas – the Chairman insisted that with the Chief Constable's permission, which he had already obtained – I was rewarded with the best selection of ties I had ever worn. Even the Sergeant got one as well!

I never did get that drink in the Chief Petty Officers' Mess that night!

CHAPTER 18

PORTHLEVEN
FISHY BUSINESS!

It was during my time as a detective constable at Helston that the then new Prime Minister and his wife, Rt. Hon. Harold Wilson MP and Mrs Mary Wilson often visited the Isles of Scilly to stay in their bungalow. It was normal for them to either take the train or drive down from London and fly to the island of St. Mary's by helicopter from RNAS *Culdrose*. I recollect that Mrs Mary Wilson wrote poems at that time and I found them of interest.

If the weather was bad, it was possible that their flight to St. Mary's would be delayed and they would have to spend time at

Newspaper report

Harbour Hotel Porthleven

the naval air station waiting for the weather to clear. Whilst they were always accompanied by a personal protection officer from the Metropolitan Police, being the local Detective Constable I was contacted. Along with the Royal Navy Master at Arms, Provost Branch and Ministry of Defence police we would ensure their privacy and safety. In fact, threats were few in those days and thankfully the base was a private and safe environment.

There were times, however when the Prime Minister would be accompanied by a friend such as Mr Frank Cousins, a trade union official. If unable to fly to St. Mary's, and caused to stay overnight in the officers' mess they would prefer a local visit away from the base to help pass the time. Local public houses in Helston were too public and we ventured into the countryside around the borough to the premises of a trusted publican. Here in a 'back room or bar' the group would sample the local ale in privacy and comfort before being returned to the base for the night. I can smell the aroma of that pipe now!

Not all cases were as amusing. I once had to interview the headmaster and headmistress of a the local Grammar School with the Detective Inspector from Truro about serious allegations of assaults on pupils. That case made the *News of the World* and was rather 'sordid'. One of the accused kept goats that made our entry to the property where she lived rather awkward. I let the Detective Inspector go first!

On another occasion, I was visiting my friend the licensee of the Harbour Inn at Porthleven, the port for Helston a few miles away on the Atlantic coast. John Knight was a brilliant artist and together we painted murals on the pub passage walls. Sadly, he too has died. He was asthmatic and died on a ferry cruise to France during a bad attack. Our families were friends and the children of similar ages. Although a publican, he was trustworthy and normally, a police officer would not befriend anyone in that trade – but our relationship was a genuine one and one that did us both good. I received a lot of information from that establishment. It was one evening that John told me he was very worried about the condition of his Great Dane, a fine animal and a boxer dog who had been examined by the veterinary surgeon with alarming results. Both had experienced anal interference. They were normally placid animals and could be approached and touched by anyone. They were kept in a large old sail loft under the archway at the back of the inn. I told John that I would keep observation from one of his downstair rooms when I could. I was doing this one evening when a small man, unknown to me – not a normal patron of the bar of the establishment - went into the adjacent barn where a fishmonger kept his portable stall and boxes. He was in there for some time so I left the observation point and entered the barn. To my amazement the man was engaged in a sexual act of bestiality with a large fish – a skate! I arrested him and John

Porthleven Harbour – fishing boat

called for transport for me with the prisoner to the police station. The man was mentally sick and when he appeared before the court he was sent for trial and placed in a suitable establishment. He had also interfered with John's dogs. This type of offence was alleged to have been very common in remote rural areas of Cornwall and Wales at the turn of the century – the 19th that is!

I mention this case to show that the unexpected can always surprise you when you least expect it. Being a detective in Cornwall was so different in the variety of offences requiring investigation. Life was never dull!

I did take my days off and often went to Loe Bar, a strand of sand and pebbles on the Atlantic coast near Portleven, or to Praa Sands (Prah Sands).We would take the two children and the poodle and enjoy a day out and pasties which I re-heated in an old cake tin on a small camping gas stove. It was not far from Helston and they knew where they could find me if I was wanted. The local policeman, Norman Pawley, renowned for his tobacco growing, knew where I went. His spare bedroom in the police house at Porthleven was his drying room. Always full of tobacco leaves in the late summer and autumn. We never knew if the Customs and Excise men knew! He certainly didn't smoke it all himself and very few smoked a pipe at the police station.

When not at the beach or out walking, I would be tending my chickens and garden at the rear of the police station. It was a lovely south facing spot with rich loam soil. Production of produce was prolific and Nicola was dwarfed by the gigantic beans, sunflowers, sweet peas and beans. The climate was perfect for growing vegetables, plenty of rain, warm sun, no wind and mild winters. The latter made the house damp but we relied on a plentiful supply of logs from one of the estates in the peninsula to keep us all warm. If the weather was bad over the peninsula we could drive to the north coast where it was invariably better. There we could wonder at the Atlantic breakers and surf crashing along the vast expanses on sandy beaches. The fresh sea air was so different from the milder south west coastal area.

The old derelict Cornish tin mines always fascinated me. Their tall chimneys marking the dangerous disused shafts and flooded tunnels below. I would often draw or paint them. There were many at nearby Wendron. The bleak landscape of the peninsula was also an artistic challenge in itself. The cliffs and coves, the images of shipwrecks of yesteryear, smugglers, fishermen, lifeboat men, farmers – all had lived or were still living on 'my patch' and inspired me in my art.

CHAPTER 19

TRAGEDIES AND HIGH NOTES!

It was whilst I was working in the garden one day I was told there had been a very bad accident on the main road from the Lizard towards Helston. A car had driven head on into a large lorry. The occupant of the car had been killed in the accident. The Sergeant informed me that it was suspicious and would like me to assist the PC dealing. He was my friend PC Laws. This I did and what transpired was a sad revelation. It appeared that a seaman had fallen in love with a WREN and she had told him that she did not want to marry him or continue the affair. Because of this we subsequently learned that he had decided to kill himself. He drove towards Helston until he saw a lorry and drove head on into it. He died instantly from his injuries. The lorry driver sustained minor injuries and shock. How I knew

Oil painting of Cornish tin mine 1964

the driver's intentions was gleaned from playing back a tape recorder found in the wreckage of the car. It had survived the accident. The driver was talking all the time he drove from the camp. You could hear his mood change from his voice and his intentions revealed at the moment before impact. You could hear the impact and then silence! It was one of the most dramatic and sad things I had to listen to. The typist cried as we transcribed the tape for the Coroner. It had to be done – in fact I finished off the transcript. It was a sad case of suicide. One of many I dealt with during my fourteen years in the Criminal Investigation Departments in Cornwall and Wiltshire.

Two days later, I returned to digging up my new potatoes, but that recorded voice could be heard in my head for many months to follow.

Not all sudden deaths were straight forward. Being a peninsula surrounded by the wild Atlantic ocean, many unfortunate people met their death by drowning, either whilst swimming, fishing or from a boat. If a body is not recovered almost immediately, it will likely return to the surface within eight to nine days and depending on the tides, return to shore miles away from the place of death and often in a decomposed or partial decomposed state. Recovery is not a pleasant task and often difficult.

On one occasion, a person had been missing at sea from Falmouth for some time and a body washed up at Mullion Cove, some forty or so nautical miles from Falmouth. It was later realised that the body had been carried by the tide and winds out into Falmouth Bay, around the Lizard Peninsula and washed inshore again near Mullion. The cove was isolated and only accessible by a steep cliff path worn by sheep. PC Staff Pedlar had dealt with the report in Falmouth of the missing person and as it happened, having once served at Mullion as a country policeman, he was only too willing to join me at Helston for the recovery. He knew the locals well.

Acrylic painting of Coastal tin mine

The coastguards gathered and recovery to the cliff top was discussed. PC Pedlar knew the farmer who owned the field immediately above the scene and that he had a horse! An old gate was found, the body – or what was left of it – placed on the gate and secured with twine. The horse was attached to the gate and with a pat on the back – it pulled the load to the cliff top via the narrow, precipitous track. (On this occasion there were no photographs!) The body was identified from dental records and the undertakers arranged cremation. Another case solved in a practical and co-operative manner!

Police marksmen have a good season

Tragedies were many, comedies were few – a sense of humour was essential to be a detective. I wouldn't describe myself as a 'hard' man by nature, but you had to be to survive the tragedies and misfortunes of others. My years were filled with sorting out other people's problems – often my own went unnoticed, lost in the devotion I had to my role as a police officer. I was an agent in my own right, yet a slave to the problems of others to the degree that I could not escape my responsibilities. Everything I did I did with total commitment. Half measures were not for me!

My only escape from duty at Helston in a semi-official capacity was my love of small bore rifle shooting. We formed

Cornwall Constabulary shooting team

a team within the Cornwall Constabulary Athletic Club, of which I was a member and with the Superintendent's and Inspector's support entered the Cornwall Small Bore League and the police National Championships. I also became a member of the National Smallbore Rifle Association. We did well in both and won cups and medals. The team comprised, PC Norman Pawley, PC Bill Pankhurst, PC Dick Osborne, PC Trevor Hill, PC Maurice Elliott, myself, (Supt. S Keast – Divisional Representative of the C.C.A.C.), Inspector J Dunn, and PC Doug Wesson. PC Bill Laws was also in the team, but not available for the photograph. I was in charge of the weapons and ammunition which together were kept in a cabinet in my office and we had free use of a private indoor shooting range in a doctor's garden at Helston. The other semi-official activity I enjoyed was being in the Cornwall Constabulary Male Voice Choir whose popularity was increasing year by year. I was with them for seven years and every concert and rehearsal was enjoyable – different venues, different programmes and a different cause. The choir continued until the late nineties when I am told it finally disbanded due to lack of support.

CHAPTER 20

SCIENTIFIC PROGRESS –
PUNISHMENT FITS THE CRIME!

The entire population of the Lizard Peninsula would remember the satellite receiving station for the GPO, known to the locals as the 'Space Station', that was built and operational in 1963 at Goonhilly Down. This was the Post Office's first satellite station, with gigantic dishes that shone in the sunlight near the Lizard Peninsula. I saw it develop from a disused air station and camp to what became the latest in transmission of signals via satellite to other parts of the globe. The opening night was watched by millions. I was there to witness the great event. Raymond Baxter of the BBC covered the event and many saw it on television. We had recently purchased a black and white Bush TV in a brown bakelite case on hire-purchase, paying monthly instalments to watch the news, children's programmes, plays and my favourite, the *Black and White Minstrel Show*. I loved the George Mitchell Singers and endeavoured never to miss a programme. Christmas specials were really special in those days and *Songs of Praise* on a Sunday became very special when we took part in a harbourside broadcast from Porthleven. "For those in Peril on the Sea" said it all!

The people, even the villains and gypsies were special in that peninsula. They all assisted me even when a gypsy was suspected of stealing corn, one told me I suspected the wrong man and pointed me in the right direction, to catch the offender, a fellow gypsy of a different family! That case resulted in me taking possession of a pair of trousers to prove that he had stolen corn from a farm. The presence of a sample taken at the laboratory in Bristol from the offender's trousers matched that unique species sown on that farm. The forensic evidence proved the case and the man pleaded guilty and was fined and made to complete a day's work on the farm! This was an early example of where my interest and desire to utilise forensic evidence in the detection of crime had worked. I often remembered that book by Bernard Spilsbury that had led me to choosing a career in the police service. There were many more examples during the remainder of my time as a detective.

In those days, villains knew where they stood with the law. The law enforcers knew what to expect when dealing with criminals in relation to the sentence. A first offender would be cautioned if they admitted the offence or prosecuted if the circumstances warranted it. The progressive nature of sentencing was known and respected by all parties involved. A juvenile would be sent to the juvenile court, placed on probation, an attendance centre, approved school and Borstal – in that order upon re-offending. The adult would expect a prison sentence for a serious offence, especially after a second appearance, then corrective training in prison and finally, preventive detention for the serious offences and repeated criminal activities. Now, there is no logical sequence in sentencing. No real deterrent as defence representatives gamble with pleas for leniency; even after hardened criminals have already been to prison. This can result in absurd decisions and I believe, punishment becomes a lottery. Bewilderment follows from both victims and offenders who cannot believe their luck, or lack of it, in the lottery of criminal activity.

CHAPTER 21

TIME TO LEAVE AND MOVE ON

During the spring of 1965, Mandy Burgess, a sergeant's wife at Helston came to see me. She drew my attention to an advertisement in the Police Review. Home Office policy had dictated that forces advertised every sixth post for promotion to outside forces. The Wiltshire Constabulary was advertising for sergeants. I was qualified and with about 70% of the Cornwall Constabulary qualified for promotion, I could wait for a long time before I was selected to be promoted.

I applied along with six hundred others from all over the country. After interview I was one of six selected.

In August 1965, we packed our furniture and belongings and transferred to Wiltshire. My time in Cornwall had come to an end. In a way I was reluctant to leave, but I knew I wanted to progress in my career and I had to go.

I left behind the many memories I have described and many more. A county of wonderful traditions and people and a grounding in police work with men and women I would never have missed and could not have bettered. It is because of those memories that I have written them for all to read. If dates are not exactly right, things are not in the exact chronological order, events are slightly muddled – then that is my 'Fuzzy Memory' If I have omitted to mention someone or got a name or place wrong – then that too is my 'Fuzzy Memory'.

In telling my story, I hope that those interested will have savoured what life was like in the constabulary in the late fifties, early sixties. To those who served with me, and are still alive - 'thank-you' – for your part in making the Cornwall Constabulary a happy experience. I can say without any doubt whatsoever, that during those years I truly felt part of a community, surrounded by true friends and my task worthwhile.